Praise for *Needy*

"*Needy* isn't just a powerfully moving book, it's a permission slip. It's permission to give yourself what you need, permission to create boundaries, permission to move through discomfort and ask for the support you crave, and permission to show up for your messy, beautiful life as your messy, beautiful self without apology or explanation."

Courtney Carver

author of *Soulful Simplicity* and *Project 333*

"This is not a self-help book. This is a call for you to step into your life, fully. A mix of science, anecdotes from her coaching life, and hard-earned wisdom, Mara invites every reader to redefine neediness and what is gained when we accept every part of our humanity. *Needy*, above all, makes room for imperfection, mess, and growth; it feels like a warm hug."

Meghan Leahy

parent coach, *Washington Post* columnist,
author of *Parenting Outside the Lines*

"This book feels like required reading for being human—both in partnership with yourself and others—in this world. Even if you've started the work of advocating for yourself, *Needy* can offer a guide and support. You will be grateful you made yourself a priority."

Cait Flanders

author of *The Year of Less* and *Adventures in Opting Out*

"*Needy* is a game changer for all of us who have lived from the belief that our needs are Too Much and, thus, we are Too Much. Mara beautifully guides us to consider that disavowing our needs serves everyone in our lives other than us and illustrates the high cost of not owning what we want, need, and desire in life. This book is a must-read!"

Victoria Albina, NP, MPH

"Let me be clear: *Needy* is a book that will be supportive to you in deeply sustainable ways. It is permission for so many of us high-functioning, recovering people pleasers to drop our swords and choose to live life a different way. This will be a book you want to give to all your friends and follow up with discussion over a cup of tea."

Becca Piastrelli
author of *Root & Ritual*

Needy

Needy

How to Advocate for Your Needs and Claim Your Sovereignty

Mara Glatzel

sounds true
BOULDER, COLORADO

Sounds True

Boulder, CO 80306

Published 2023

Book design by Charli Barnes

Printed in the United States of America

BK06507

Library of Congress Cataloging-in-Publication Data

Names: Glatzel, Mara, author.
Title: Needy : how to advocate for your needs and claim your sovereignty / Mara Glatzel.
Description: Boulder, CO : Sounds True, 2023. | Includes bibliographical references.
Identifiers: LCCN 2022021984 (print) | LCCN 2022021985 (ebook) | ISBN 9781683649847 (hardcover) | ISBN 9781683649854 (ebook)
Subjects: LCSH: Self-actualization (Psychology) | Self-reliance.
Classification: LCC BF637.S4 G555 2023 (print) | LCC BF637.S4 (ebook) | DDC 158.1--dc23/eng/20220825
LC record available at https://lccn.loc.gov/2022021984
LC ebook record available at https://lccn.loc.gov/2022021985

10 9 8 7 6 5 4 3 2 1

FSC
www.fsc.org
MIX
Paper | Supporting
responsible forestry
FSC® C103098

For Delphina and Freya,
May you know what you need in order to thrive
and have the courage to ask for it.

You do not have to be good.

You do not have to walk on your knees

For a hundred miles through the desert, repenting.

You only have to let the soft animal of your body

love what it loves.

Tell me about despair, yours, and I will tell you mine.

Meanwhile the world goes on.

Meanwhile the sun and the clear pebbles of the rain

are moving across the landscapes,

over the prairies and the deep trees,

the mountains and the rivers.

Meanwhile the wild geese, high in the clean blue air,

are heading home again.

Whoever you are, no matter how lonely,

the world offers itself to your imagination,

calls to you like the wild geese, harsh and exciting—

over and over announcing your place

in the family of things.

—"WILD GEESE" BY MARY OLIVER[1]

Contents

ii

Contents

You're Needy, and I Love That About You

This book is for humans who have needs, especially those of us who pretend we don't.

This book is for those of us who are longing for something we can't even name.

This book is for those of us who are overwhelmed and those of us who are just one yes away from complete and utter burnout.

This book is for those of us who believe that what we do makes us infinitely more interesting and worthy than who we are.

This book is for those of us who are preoccupied by mentally scanning every room we walk into and anticipating every need around us.

This book is for those of us who learned to mask our needs under an armor of self-reliance because our needs weren't met as children.

This book is for those of us who don't often feel seen, held, or heard.

This book is for those of us trying to tend to our needs in the hidden corners of our lives to protect ourselves from the intimacy of having our messy humanity witnessed and judged.

This book is for those of us who carry the story that no one would stay if they really knew us.

This book is for those of us who abandon ourselves in an attempt to belong.

I FELT MY FRUSTRATION RISING UP from the pit of my stomach as my partner and I made our schedule for the week. My partner outlined their needs—the hours their business required of them, the classes at the gym they wanted to take to feel good in their body, and the lunch adventure to a local restaurant they hoped we'd take as a new family. I wanted to be supportive, but as I listened, I felt consumed by a familiar swell of anger and resentment.

Barely four months after the birth of our first child, my neediness felt like a pot boiling over, and I'd never had less personal time or space to figure things out. I was accustomed to shielding my true self from the humans around me for fear of overwhelming them, a lesson learned from a lifetime of being told I was too much—too ambitious, too big, too loud, too many feelings, too many needs—plus the steady social conditioning of what a good woman should be. I had learned to tend to myself in the shadowy corners of my day, during the infrequent moments when my to-do list was complete and no one else needed me.

Somewhere along the way, I learned to believe that minimizing my needs was what it meant to be a good wife, friend, mother, coach, sister, and daughter because that image was reflected back at me from the heavy onslaught of media messaging, but it was deeper than that too. Many of my adolescent role models diverged from this ideal, but I rejected them as outliers in a pursuit for unconditional belonging.

I wanted to be liked. I wanted to be seen as good, as worthy. I wanted to fit in. I wanted the safety that I assumed homogeneity would give me. And so, I groomed myself in this way, strictly monitoring myself in an attempt to keep the peace and make other people comfortable, even when it meant that I, myself, was uncomfortable. This messaging felt unimpeachably true because the reminders were mirrored back to me from every angle—take care of yourself, don't make a fuss, be chill, downplay your feelings, be good. Be less, so that someone else will find you attractive. Keep yourself safe from rejection or abandonment. Somewhere along the way, I learned to believe that making myself invisible in this way was necessary in order to secure the love and belonging I ached for.

But in that moment on the couch, I could feel the hot shame of my neediness flooding me and threatening to eat me up whole. I felt angry when I thought of how unsupported I felt, but I didn't have the vocabulary to describe how I wanted to be supported. I was so exhausted. I needed a shower. I was ashamed that I couldn't smooth myself over and smile and nod graciously the way I had practiced for so long. My new postpartum body felt foreign. I desperately wanted to have the space and energy to return to my work. And my partner was taking everything—all of the available time, space, and shared resources. Intellectually I knew this wasn't true, but it *felt* true. It felt as though we were fighting over one tiny scrap of available time, and they were grabbing it and leaving me with nothing.

Suddenly, I exploded, "Why are the things you want to do nonnegotiable? What about MY things? What about MY needs?" Tears rolled down my face as I got tangled up between needing to ask for something and feeling as though I didn't even have the time or energy to figure out what it was. In spite of myself, I was quickly becoming that thing I tried really hard not to be—needy.

Surprised, my partner calmly replied, "If there are things that you want and need to do, you need to ask for them. It is not my job to read your mind. And when you say you are going to do something, you have to safeguard it. It's not my fault that you keep giving all of your time away."

Those words stung. I felt so angry, and while I wanted to be angry at them, really, I was angry at myself. When had I stopped mattering? Why was I so quick to make myself small in order to take care of everyone else? Why did I believe that asking for help made me a burden? The truth was, I hadn't prioritized my care. I hadn't respected my limits or set boundaries to protect my energy. I hadn't advocated for my needs. I hadn't even allowed myself to acknowledge that I had needs.

Somewhere along the way, I had abandoned myself.

I was longing to feel understood and valued, and I wanted them to do that for me. I wanted them to acknowledge my hard work and self-sacrifice with gifts, ample words of affirmation, and permission to tend to myself in whatever frivolous way occurred to me, but really, underneath all of that, I wanted to matter.

The profound ache of this desire ran much deeper than what was happening in my relationship. When I started to trace it back, I found the need woven throughout the entire fabric of my life, braided into every relational pattern I had learned was necessary to belong. I had shielded others from the fullest and truest expression of myself for as long as I could remember, spending my life squeezing into the small boxes I created for myself and believing this uncomfortable restriction was a necessary apology for my too-muchness.

As a fat, loud, smart, and opinionated human with a lot of feelings, I was and am kind of a handful—something that I have learned to adore about myself after an adolescence littered with bullying and experiences of being told I should be ashamed of who I was because of the size of my body, the bright tenacity of my ambition, and my natural appetite for growth in every direction. *I am too much*, I told myself over and over—too many words, too many feelings, too many interests, too many desires. I carried these lessons through to adulthood, reliving them each time I tried to bend myself into shapes to earn external approval, feel loved, or belong to the humans that surrounded me. Often I did this by making sure the needs of those around me were met and I was earning my worthiness one carefully perfected step at a time.

Like many of us, my automatic association with having my own needs was negative.

"Don't be needy!"

But, what is neediness apart from a bid for connection? Neediness is the presence of a desire to matter, a deep yearning to be prioritized and handled with care. Your needs—and mine—were never the problem, even as our social understanding of them is littered with examples of disposable, unlovable, unworthy, clingy, too-much humans. Hungry ghosts who are never satisfied. People who are a profound drag to be in a relationship with or who you often hear are dumped or rejected. Our needs are not the problem, but they become more challenging to hold— both for us and the people around us—when they are not addressed, verbalized, or well tended. They become more challenging to hold when we endeavor to outsource them to the people around us because we were never given the tools to tend to them ourselves and because we were taught that minimizing our needs was an act of love and service to those around us. The less our needs are met, the more frantic we become to get them met, by whatever means necessary, because we are humans and humans have needs. We require care. This is an unshakeable fact.

I was, and am, needy. We all are. And yet, at that point in my life, I had never taken the time to get to know what my needs were, an ignorance fueled by the belief that being needy was bad and not burdening other people with my needs was good. I knew it was better to rise above and overcome them. I had learned I felt safest when I tucked myself in, hiding my messiest truths from view. And because I had never really risked sharing my needs with anyone, they often went unmet.

The presence of those unmet needs fueled a belief that no one cared what I needed, that my needs didn't matter, and that I should meet them myself when possible and ignore them when that was not possible. I knew no matter how small and cramped I felt inside the little box I had created around myself, it felt infinitely more dangerous to let myself out.

Lost in the abyss of a life that didn't reflect me, I became accustomed to doing what was expected of me as quickly as possible, and never stopped to ask myself what I wanted or needed. One day I found myself surrounded by people who did not truly know me, as I busily moved around a life I didn't recognize.

On the outside it looked great—prestigious graduate degree, attractive fiancé, busy in preparation for a perfect vineyard wedding. I was a high-functioning individual who received a lot of praise for her efforts. I was excellent at not needing anything from anyone and was relentlessly reliable.

And I was *miserable*.

I felt wholly disconnected from my body and was teeming with resentment over the many, many trespasses upon boundaries I had never expressed—the moments when my body was offered up for public opinion, the feelings I squashed in an effort to make my friends happy, and the way I dimmed my own shine in an attempt to keep myself safe by keeping others comfortable. My entire life was set up for other people to think I was doing a good job, and I had zero understanding about replenishing the energy that doing a good job was costing me.

This worked for me for a long, long time—right up until it explicitly and definitively didn't.

And so began the long process of acknowledging the depth of my own self-abandonment. With time, I realized nothing in my life was free from needing to be examined in this new light. From the shift I made away from the career in social work I almost pursued, right up to the conversation about caring for my needs that I had with my partner, this work quickly became about whether or not I was actually willing to allow myself to be who and how I was—regardless of how I was received by others. It was humbling to realize how much of my power I had been giving away while waiting for someone else to tell me I had earned the tending I ached for. This is a lesson I anticipate learning again a hundred times in my lifetime.

The work in this book is work I myself have done and continue to do. It's tender and challenging, maybe in a different way from anything you've ever done before. And it is so very worth it.

From Safety to Celebration

How did you find your way to the margins of your own life? So many of us find our way there, one way or another. And it always, always comes back to needs. How did your needs get pushed to the periphery—tucked away for a better, more convenient or ideal moment that never seems to arrive? Do you, in fact, know what you need to begin with?

Let's take a moment to define what needs actually are. A need is something you *require* in order to exist and thrive. Human bodies, minds, and hearts have needs. There is no escaping this, even in a world where we are so often forced to abandon our needs if we want to succeed or belong to the status quo. You also have wants. A want is something you *desire* in order to exist and thrive. A want takes your particular hunger for engagement and personal predilections into account, allowing you to meet your needs in a way that is both unique to you and particularly satisfying for you to receive. When it comes to considering your needs and wants, it can be tempting to try to put them into a hierarchy. I lovingly urge you not to do this. It might feel as though you barely have the energy or ability to focus on your needs while a want feels much too big or scary, but both are essential for occupying the full breadth of your life with pleasure, satisfaction, and deep enjoyment. This is a stretch for many of us—a good one. I encourage you to lean into that expansion as much as you can while reading this book, inviting yourself to fully occupy your body and your life to the best of your abilities. Yes, this is a book about identifying, honoring, and advocating for your needs, but at its core, this is a book about you welcoming more of yourself into your life and giving both your needs *and* your wants space to take form and flourish.

Everything you do, from the moment you wake up to the moment you go to bed, is a choice made to meet a need, whether you realize it or not. The more you can understand the vocabulary of your needs and develop a relationship with yourself that allows you to be present with what is—no matter what—the more consciously you will meet those needs. This will enable you to better ally with yourself, freeing yourself from judgment as you approach yourself with great compassion.

When you think about your needs now, you might feel familiar with your body's physical needs for air, food, water, rest, nourishment, and shelter. This book aims to grow that understanding, building your vocabulary to encompass your mental, emotional, spiritual, and energetic needs as well. There are universal needs we all experience—the need for safety, rest, sustenance, trust, integrity, sovereignty, love, belonging, and celebration, for example—but each of us experiences them in our own way, which is why reconnecting with yourself is an essential skill for this work.

What are the consequences of not addressing your needs? They are myriad—and I am certain that if you are reading this book you are already familiar with some of them. You might be experiencing a diminished excitement for your life, a heightened presence of anger or resentment, or a felt sense that you aren't receiving the same care you routinely offer others. You might feel unhappy or unappreciated in your relationships or feel secretly hungry for changes that seem impossible to ask for. You might carry the weight of not wanting to be a burden, even as you feel increasingly fraught or overwhelmed. You might be living a life in which you don't see your truest self reflected. Your needs might be shifting because of life circumstances or hormonal changes that cause your current body to feel foreign to you. You might be tense, chronically ill, fatigued, or facing a major health crisis—but still attempting to push yourself forward in an effort to keep up. You might be bending yourself into shapes to keep the people in your life comfortable—but all the while be navigating profound bouts of discomfort.

Stacey and I began working together after a difficult conversation she'd had with her daughter about how her daughter felt pressure to suppress her needs for Stacey to be okay. Her daughter admitted that during her childhood she felt like she had to express gratitude and love for her mother during her mother's lowest moments, and at times she had secretly resented that. During this conversation, Stacey felt bitterly angry when confronted with what she heard as her daughter's judgment of her doing the best she could during a challenging time—anger that provided a more comfortable cover for the shame and confusion she felt about her behavior. Wasn't it her daughter's job to appreciate her, Stacey wondered? At the same time, she recognized that she wanted her daughter to feel unconditionally loved and free to ask for what she needed—even when it hurt Stacey to face her percieved inadequacies directly.

Stacey's plight urges us to think about what we do with our "ugly" needs. The ones that are painful to hold and grow through. The ones that keep us from the very relationships we deeply desire. The ones that we never learned to express, even to ourselves. Through our work together, I reminded Stacey that all needs are neutral. No need is shameful. But the way that we learn to outsource our needs to people we are in relationship with can be hurtful, smothering, overwhelming, or burdensome. When Stacey felt overextended and burned-out, she needed everyone around her to love and approve of her, to make her feel okay by expressing gratitude for her efforts; otherwise, she would begin feeling resentful. This pattern wasn't fair to her daughter, and it wasn't fair to Stacey not to appreciate herself by setting boundaries around her available time and energy. By giving more than she truly had to offer, Stacey had secretly set up a transactional interaction with her daughter. Stacey routinely trespassed her own boundaries around what she had to offer, giving more than she had to give and feeling her child owed her for her efforts.

The questions remain. How do we lovingly confront long-standing patterns while remaining on our own side? How do we tenderly hold the shame that gets excavated when we realize we've been trying to get our needs met in ways that are hurtful, harmful, or oppressive to the people around us? This wasn't Stacey's intention—although that was the impact. When Stacey was able to hold her own hand through her discomfort, she was also able to figure out how to address her needs and advocate for them instead of expecting the people around her to read her mind.

Journal prompts to dive deeper:

What are the costs of neglecting my needs?

Who benefits from me suppressing my needs?

How do I benefit from suppressing my needs?

What are the risks I imagine will crop up as I delve into welcoming more of my needs into my life?

It can be challenging to imagine what might be on the other side of this work if you are in the thick of navigating the consequences of not having your needs met. This book aims to cast a vision of what might be possible for you as you begin weaving a greater sense of your needs into your life. What might it feel like to have these tender and true parts of you not only acknowledged but also prioritized? How might you relax into your relationships if you felt rooted in a deep sense of self-partnership? What would you strive for if you trusted yourself to be kind and compassionate no matter the outcome? What would you ask for if you no longer saw your needs as a flaw or a burden?

The best way I can describe the other side of this work is the enormous exhalation it brings and the unshakeable confidence of knowing there is no one else and nowhere else you should be. You are able to exist as the human you are because the presence of your humanity no longer negates your self-worth. Will it be perfect? No. There will be many moments when things are uncomfortable and challenging—but you will feel certain that those experiences don't mean you're doing anything wrong.

It's important for you to know that no matter how far in the margins you find yourself, you always have permission to abandon that course of action and to restructure your life by bringing yourself to the center of it. At the crux of this rebuilding and learning to identify, honor, and advocate for your needs are both the truth that you *are* needy and that you have full, unbridled, and inexplicable permission to be that way. I will not tell you that you deserve to have your needs met (you do) or that you are worthy of them (you are), because their existence is a fact, not a flaw.

You live in a world that doesn't provide for or honor your needs, but that doesn't mean there is something wrong with you for having them. These pages have been written with the express purpose of inviting this thick, life-affirming permission back into your body to take up residence there. You are your own responsibility and belonging to yourself is your birthright. You have permission to grow your relationship with yourself from self-abandonment to self-partnership, no matter how many times you've broken your own promises before or how untrustworthy you fear you are.

Being in relationship with yourself isn't something you do once and then set on a shelf in your closet to forget about. Much like building a strong and enduring relationship with another person, being in relationship with yourself requires your attention, commitment, care, and devotion.

This work is an intentionally slow process. The path home to yourself isn't about racing toward an ultimate destination of perfection, where all of your problems are magically solved or you never experience any amount of struggle again. Instead, it is about journeying with yourself at your own side. A relationship brimming with self-love isn't created through flash-in-the-pan, one-size-fits-all self-care plans. It is created with patience, kindness, and presence, and all it asks of you is that you do the best you can.

I—possibly like you—have spent many, many years wanting the answer to be something else. I have been so exhausted that a quick fix felt like the only thing I had the capacity for. The daily commitment of remaining at my own side has sometimes felt daunting, like an insurmountable mountain of undesired responsibility. There is a part of me that STILL wants it to be easier, even as I know that the answer I am looking for always returns to the real, responsive self-care that I share in this book.

> Do less, more often.

> Move slower.

> It's uncomfortable, and you'll always wonder if you're doing enough. You are.

> Keep going.

This work is uncomfortable because learning how to partner with yourself in your discomfort IS the work—figuring out what tools you have when things are tricky or unclear, understanding what you need when you are feeling excruciatingly human, and learning how to tend to yourself with increasing nuance and specificity.

Unlearning Your Way to Self-Partnership

This book is part prayer and part experiment in imagination, in which an aspect of taking radical responsibility for our needs means centering ourselves in our own minds, lives, and joy—regardless of where society tells us our mattering falls on its hierarchy of value. While I am aware that this work cannot and should not take the place of structural change, I am curious about how oppression is braided into our relationship with ourselves and then recreated in daily choices about our needs. I am curious how we might reclaim these daily choices as testaments to our inherent worthiness and with time teach ourselves what it means to be valued, EVEN AS we continue to exist in a world that does not value us.

This unlearning is lifelong work as we continue to unearth systems that undermine our self-trust, cause us to feel distant and detached from our bodies, and condition us to believe we aren't allowed to receive the tenderness and pleasure we ache for. If you have ever told yourself that you are a failure or that your neediness is a personal weakness, which hasn't allowed you to trust yourself, please hear me when I tell you that it is not your fault. No matter what happened before, now is a perfectly good time to start unlearning beliefs that keep you small and second-guessing your phenomenal capacity for making positive change in your life and the world around you. It is easy to lose yourself in a world of noise and pressure. You might be overwhelmed with options, tantalized by pixels promising that if you hand yourself over to the next thing—fix, diet, program, or product—you will be healed or somehow magically become better than you are now.

Or maybe you grew up in a family with a legacy around worthi-ness and belonging passed down through generations that causes you to believe that you are valuable only when you offer every last drop of energy without any thought for your own replenishment. Maybe you were raised in a society that told you in no uncertain terms that you were most lovable when you were the least complicated, when you were easily digestible and not in the slightest bit needy. Or maybe all of those conditions and more have been piled up, one upon the other, until you forgot it was even possible to befriend yourself as you are now attempting to do.

Unlearning your social conditioning requires uprooting the beliefs that prevent you from befriending yourself and attending to your humanity with reverence—and that's exactly what this book is about.

Your body is sacred land. This unlearning is a call to return to who you really are inside. It is an invitation to realign with the soft animal of your body as you learn to shed the social being you were conditioned to become in order to get ahead, succeed, and "get your needs met." A deli-ciously nourishing and sustainable life requires attending to your needs and wants while simultaneously disentangling from the conditioning that keep you from feeling you deserve this attention from yourself. This book seeks to reunite you with your body, guiding you down a path of unlearning what you've been taught about your needs in order to reconnect you with your truest essential self. And this includes what you may have been taught about self-care.

Needs, Identities, and Systems of Oppression

I am writing this book from the perspective of a White, fat, queer, femme mother of two, who was raised in a lower-class family at the tip of Cape Cod in Massachusetts, the unceded homelands of the Wampanoag Nation and Paomet Wampanoag people. My father is a German immigrant, and my mother is a fourth-generation Italian American. I have a master's degree in social work and have been working for myself for the last ten years as a coach, a writer, and a podcast host. In offering this work, it is essential for me to own that a White woman like myself is protected by privilege and benefits from that privilege—a fact that has nothing to do with the worthiness of my needs and everything to do with the systems of oppression our culture is steeped in.

And also, as a fat woman, my understanding of my value has been shaped by the systems and humans I have come into contact with over the course of my life, as well as my own internalization of those systems.

Every time I had a doctor who prioritized the size of my body over my health, every time I went to a fitness class where the instructor assumed I wasn't flexible or able to do the poses, every time I searched for a winter coat only to find my size wasn't available, and every time someone made an assumption about my worth based on their perception of my appearance, I absorbed these perceptions as if they were true about me. How could they not be? They were reflected back to me from every angle. I was taught that my body was bad and that I was bad by extension.

When I say "bad" here, I am referring to the value others gave the appearance of my body. Discussions about the functionality of my physical self, my needs, my pleasure, my health, my joy, or how my body felt to me were put on hold as something that would happen for me on the other side of losing weight, when I was determined worthy of them. And because I was never successful in a wholesale changing of my body to fit the ideals set for me, there was always something deep inside of me that felt as though I needed to apologize or make up for it. In some ways, all of the stories in this book are about my grappling with this exact thing— trying to earn my goodness in order to meet my needs for safety and belonging, because I was taught that I was flawed if my body was flawed and that no one would want me unless I gave them a really good reason.

Human Needs versus Systems of Oppression

It is impossible to disentangle these experiences of oppression based on my body size from the unearned advantage I carry as a White, straight-passing human with moderate financial access and education. Like many of us who embody disparate levels of access and privilege, my understanding of myself, my worth, and my needs are bound by the intersections of these identities.

The flat truth is that we live in a world where having your humanity regarded and getting your needs met are a privilege. To understand the obstacles that stand between us and getting our needs met, we must consider the ways in which systemic oppression and violence, patriarchal messaging, and privilege each impact our access to and ability to advocate for ourselves. We do not all have the same twenty-four hours in the day, and we were not all raised with the same care. Our social conditioning determines how we are taught to define ourselves, what we consider possible, and what we learn is appropriate and acceptable to ask for—as well as how we need to be to keep ourselves safe, emotionally and physically.

All human bodies, minds, and hearts have needs—and yet, historically, Black, Indigenous, and people of color have been stripped of their humanity, bodily integrity, creativity, curiosity, and needs for White people to get their needs met. The system of "care" has been built upon the labor—physical, mental, and emotional—of Black and Brown people.

Every single one of us, regardless of the intersections of our identities, cannot underestimate the way our value is reflected back to us from the world around us and then internalized as we learn to reenact these systems in our relationships with ourselves, our needs, and what we allow ourselves to ask for. You'll need to work to bring your attention to the ways in which you have embodied these harsh lessons and how they play out in the most subtle decisions each day. The inner work you do while you read the following pages is not a substitute for much needed systemic change, but it might be a prerequisite for engaging sustainably with the social and political advocacy born from your increasingly urgent understanding of the impact of such inequality.

To take ownership of our needs and responsibility for the felt experience of our lives, we must both acknowledge the impact structural oppression has on our relationship with our needs and consider how we might begin to divest from the systems of oppression we have embodied, systems that keep us from being in relationship with ourselves in ways that enable us to feel held and whole. It is my hope that this book ignites a spark of remembering for someone who might harbor a deep-seated shame, fear, belief, or lived experience that they are disposable because their needs haven't been met or their bodily dignity hasn't been respected because of their race, sexual orientation, gender-identity, body size, age, religion, or ability.

For humans reading this book who have been historically and systemically marginalized:

We live in a world that tells you directly and indirectly you don't matter and your needs don't matter. This book seeks to remind you that not only do you matter but also your needs matter tremendously. Your needs matter whether or not they have ever been met before. This work will urge you to unravel the ways you may have embodied and incorporated systems of oppression into your relationship with yourself and your relationships with the people around you. I believe that our deep understanding of and collective assertion of needs are critical to dismantling oppressive and exploitative systems. But it would be careless to gloss over the truth that there can be significant risks to advocating for your needs as a person who has experienced systemic marginalization.

As a White, cisgender, and straight-passing woman, I am well aware that this text may not be the best resource or the most pertinent lens for those who are not White, cisgender, or straight-passing. I have not lived experiences outside of these identities, and this book might not be the most appropriate resource for all identities. For this reason, at the back of the book I have included a reading list filled with expansive perspectives and embodied experiences of care. This doesn't mean you aren't welcome here—you very much are. I share these resources because I want to best serve you and connect you with whatever you need to honor your needs with a growing sense of confidence and support.

For humans reading this book who have not been historically marginalized, or whose privilege includes intersections of being White, cisgender, non-disabled, or heterosexual:

Your ability to be in touch with your needs and believe you matter is deeply personal and impacted by the capitalist, patriarchal, ageist, ableist, and White supremacist world we live in, with its collective glorification of a perfectionistic standard you will never be able to meet. Having privilege doesn't mean this work will be easy for you, though it does mean you have an unearned advantage approaching it.

You have needs, no matter where you are in the fabric of social hierarchy. Not getting your needs met negatively impacts everyone around you, and if you, like me, are a White person with an unearned advantage, it impacts the people below you in the hierarchy the most. This doesn't mean it doesn't impact your partner, friends, coworkers, or your children. It means that systemically it affects those outside your immediate circle too. Part of your work here is to take responsibility for your needs so that you stop outsourcing them to the people around you who hold marginalized identities.

The more human you allow yourself to be, the more humanity you will allow and actively encourage in others. This is one way we collectively break the tethers of supremacy that exists within us, by cultivating a deep reverence for our shared humanity—skin, bone, blood, hunger, and the yearning for belonging, joy, and community. The more space you create in your life for your own neediness, the less of a strain your needs will be on the people around you.

Real Self-Care Is Responsive, Not Prescriptive

The last couple of years have heralded an age of self-care. Articles, listicles, gurus, programs, and products are being sold everywhere to help us engage in time spent rejuvenating and restoring ourselves. This industry is responding to our collective exhaustion, burnout, and neediness, but it is continually missing the mark.

At its core, *Needy* is a book about caring for yourself. However, the self-care I describe in these pages is unlike the pristine rituals displayed in beautifully curated Instagram posts. The self-care I am referring to is the work of building an honest, trustworthy, and loving relationship with yourself, a relationship rooted in meeting your needs on a consistent basis. This relationship is the foundation beneath your feet. It is the heart of everything you do, and it grows and gets stronger each time you refuse to abandon yourself, no matter what.

Developing this relationship requires a nuanced understanding of what you need and how tending to those needs impacts your energetic capacity. The presence of your needs isn't a sign of weakness or a moral failing; it is an undeniable characteristic of living in a human body. If we are going to take better care of ourselves, we must intimately understand, acknowledge, and honor our needs. This means turning toward the wounded and vulnerable parts of ourselves and shedding light on what we ache for specifically.

This work can be difficult. Sometimes I wonder why anyone would want to take it on. But the truth is that partnering with myself saved my life. It rescued me from deep burnout and adrenal fatigue, a string of intimate relationships in which my body was not revered or respected, and a profound lack of self-trust and standard of perfectionism that held my greatest contributions hostage. This work carried me from muscling through and hating myself to a life overflowing with pauses and intentional choices.

Throughout the pages of this book, I will take a stand for the beauty of your humanity and your needs. But really, it's less about your needs being beautiful in and of themselves and more about the beautiful partnership you create with yourself when you're willing to be with what is.

I wrote this book for the little girl inside of me afraid to say what she was really hungry for, for the teenager who believed that getting the grade was the only way to survive, for the college student told she was too fat and needy to take up space, and for the mother on the couch desperate for a shower.

This is a book for humans who have lost their way and are ready to find the path back home to themselves. That sounds cliché, but it is also true. It is also a book for humans who are realizing they can no longer organize their lives in accordance with what they believe is expected of them, what they think they should do, or who they think they should be—humans who are ready to carve out a path to do things their own way and on their own terms, even if that feels scary or impossible right now.

But mostly, this is a book about claiming your undisputed sovereignty and giving yourself permission to take up space in the center of your life. It turns out my life purpose isn't to be as small, silent, and accommodating as possible—and yours isn't either.

I wrote this book in celebration of our muchness, yours and mine. This book is a guide for becoming, once and for all, the one person in your life you will never ever be too much for.

Before you turn the next page say this aloud to yourself:

> *I matter. My needs matter. I am allowed to have needs. My needs are my responsibility. I am committed to showing up—reading one page and then another, taking one loving action and then another. I do not have to do it all. I do not have to do this perfectly. All I have to do is give myself permission to BE myself—to love what I love, need what I need, and want what I want.*

CHAPTER 1

The Needy Framework

DESPITE WHAT THE SELF-HELP SECTION of the bookstore may say, there is no one-size-fits-all journey to self-love. Each of us is unique, with our own set of life circumstances, identities, privileges, tender spots, and strengths. But through my own self-healing and my work supporting thousands of humans learning to identify, honor, and advocate for their needs, I have begun to see some general themes emerge—not so much a roadmap as a human-wide pattern of behaviors and transformations people go through doing this work.

It starts (and ends) with *self-acceptance.*

Many people mistakenly believe self-acceptance means you stop growing, stop working, and stop creating. But self-acceptance simply means you're willing to coexist with the reality of your life and make peace with yourself as you are—separating your goodness and worthiness from your daily experience. You don't have to love everything about yourself. You don't even have to like everything about yourself. Instead, self-acceptance asks you to **be with** your truth rather than berate yourself for not being better already or escape to a well-conditioned fantasy of who you think you should be.

Once the grounding of self-acceptance is in place (again, be it ever so tenuously), growth starts to happen in four iterative and consecutive stages:

> **Self-responsibility:** Cultivating awareness of who you are, what you stand for, and what you need. At this stage, you are accepting responsibility for your own care, education, and perhaps most importantly, your role in unlearning the beliefs, societal messaging, and dominant narratives you have embodied that cause you harm or diminish your sense of self.

Self-care: Much more than scented candles and bubble baths, this stage is about taking action to support yourself as you navigate your daily life. Resist the urge to define your readiness as the absence of fear or discomfort; instead, meet yourself within your discomfort by doing what is doable. Remain by your own side and commit to responding to how you feel and what you need, even if you're not sure what is "right" or "best" to do.

Self-trust: Trust is built through awareness, action, increased intimacy and closeness with self, dependability, self-kindness, and compassionate self-talk. Returning to these practices again and again fosters the knowledge that you will remain by your own side. Trust can be rebuilt, no matter where you've traveled or how long it's been.

Self-love: This stage refers to the brave, chewy, unconditional love that blooms from sustained self-trust, self-respect, admiration, and adoration of self. Self-love is grown through imperfect action, relentless self-support, and self-gratitude.

Throughout this book, I will offer action steps that correspond with each of these stages, as well as prompts on how to advocate for your needs in your relationships. Overall, however, this book will focus most closely on cultivating connection and partnership in your relationship with yourself. This is not because the advocacy doesn't matter—of course it does. Nevertheless, advocating for your needs requires an innate understanding of what you need, familiarity with the particular flavor of how you would best like that need met, and a deep well of self-acceptance and permission as you strive to bring this work into your relationships. The skills of self-partnership are essential for learning how to honor your needs with greater confidence and strength.

What does this look like in practice?

Radical responsibility informs your self-care and rebuilds trust. The consistency and stability of that trust eventually grows into self-love. At some point in showing up for your needs and getting to know yourself, you will feel yourself soften into a place of acceptance and love for yourself. You will learn to appreciate yourself for everything you are, and you will forgive yourself for everything that you are not.

It is important to remember that this love is not for perfect people somewhere out there, people who have their shit together more than you do. Rather, it is the love that grows from realizing the only other person in here is you and then appreciating the hell out of yourself for continuing to show up, no matter how many times you've been knocked down or cast aside. This is enduring love. It is the ancient love of knowing every nook and cranny of your inner landscape and making peace with its disappointments and idiosyncrasies. It is the love from cultivating a profound friendship with yourself, held tight with boundaries that enable you to thrive, with permission to be exactly who you are, and the brave choice to bring the fullest expression of yourself to every aspect of your life.

You will find you cycle through each of the four stages in both micro and macro ways as you find your way home to yourself. Envision this framework as a supportive structure you will fill in and make your own—or as a roadmap showing you how to cultivate a relationship with yourself so that you feel met, seen, heard, held, and life-changingly supported.

Radical Self-Responsibility

Everything that I am, need, and want is mine to tend.

Everything I have learned is true about me is
mine to explore, reject, unlearn, or hold close.

I am clear about what is mine to own and what is not.

Radical responsibility exists in the realm before and during responsive action. It is the commitment to grow from self-abandonment to self-partnership by getting to know yourself, caring for yourself as if you are worth caring for, actively building self-trust, and learning to like yourself.

Your healing and nourishment are your work, and it matters deeply. It is no longer sustainable to ignore yourself, attempt to outsource your needs, or wait until someone reads your mind. Your job as the tender steward of your life is to care for yourself with as much consistency as you can reasonably muster.

You might be reading this and thinking, *Yikes! Responsibility right off the bat? That feels heavy. I don't really want to take responsibility for myself. I'm too tired to take anything else on.* I completely understand. However, the reason you are too exhausted to tend to yourself is rooted in not knowing how or refusing to take responsibility for yourself, your care, and your needs.

In the following chapters, I will repeatedly ask you to honor your needs here and now. I will urge you to honor your needs no matter how you feel about yourself or your body on any given day. I will reiterate this truth again and again: Your tending is not optional. Your needs are not suggestions. Your requirements for living are not too big, unwieldy, or complicated to matter.

In asking you to jump straight into practicing daily care, I explicitly ask you to experiment with making promises to yourself and following through—because this is how you earn back your trust and teach yourself what it is like to be loved. The love I am referring to here is a verb. Without accountability and action, it is the toothless placation of someone who acts like your friend to your face but has no intention of showing up for your breakfast date. Make a commitment to stop being that friend to yourself here and now.

Radical self-responsibility takes YOU into account, because when it comes to tending to your life, YOU are all that matters. There is no "right" or "wrong" way—there is only what you need and how you show up for that need in a way that is sustainable and kind.

Radical self-responsibility is about stacking small actions, small well-chosen moments, until they begin to accumulate and turn into a profound support network of comprehensive care and self-appreciation.

But mostly, radical self-responsibility is about reminding yourself that you require care and that requiring care is not a deep, dark, shameful secret. Requiring care doesn't make you weak or unworthy. Reclaim your rightful place in the center of your own life and practice remaining present with yourself, no matter what shows up.

Self-Care

I require care.

It is safe to require care.

It is safe to receive care.

Imperfect action is more than enough.

The water is pooling upon the surface of the brittle, cracked earth again. You forgot to water it, and then days passed while you were busy tending to other things. When you finally got around to it, you found the soil hardened and impenetrable. You wondered if watering was even worth the effort.

It can be challenging to receive when you have been going without, steeling yourself and building walls to block the achy protest of your needs. You might "rest," but while you are resting, you are beating yourself up for being lazy and unable to get more done. You find you are more exhausted after resting than you were before, so why bother? You might try to clear a day for your own care, only to find you have no idea what to do with yourself, a feeling so challenging you load your schedule again to avoid having to deal with it.

You are the brittle earth, and you are the watering can.

You thrive with consistent, tender care. You want your needs to matter, but you haven't been showing up to do the damn thing you hunger for. Everything feels too baked in and stuck. Your needs and wants feel hazy and untrustworthy. It feels easier to just keep moving than to slow down and let it all catch up with you.

This is why traditional self-care doesn't soothe the ache. It pools on the surface, and it can be a struggle to get past our initial disappointment when it didn't work perfectly and immediately, creating a pattern of not caring for ourselves. We try to gulp from a firehose of care when care is urgently needed and then blame ourselves for not being able to receive the piecemeal care we offer ourselves.

Self-care is about healing what is keeping us stuck and disconnected from ourselves by taking the time to patiently check in with ourselves and respond to whatever feelings or needs present themselves. If you are unwilling to challenge the beliefs that underpin a life that is so busy you don't have time to hydrate yourself, it doesn't matter how many life hacks for drinking more water you learn. Self-care is about asking yourself: *What do I need to bring the fullest, most alive version of myself to this day? What does my body need from me? How can I meet these needs in a way that is DOABLE for me today?*

When it comes to our own care, something is always, always, always better than nothing. This is how we replenish our own brittle earth consistently and sustainably—one drop at a time.

Self-Trust

Rebuilding self-trust doesn't require
perfection, it requires presence.

I am committed to earning my own trust over time.

I am patient in my pursuit of self-partnership.

Consistent care and action breeds self-trust. Each moment, word uttered, and action taken has the potential either to repair or damage self-trust. Self-trust is regenerative, growing and responding as we learn to partner with ourselves with greater and greater reliability. We build trust in our relationship with ourselves the same way we build trust in a relationship with someone else, by showing up and refusing to abandon the relationship when things get messy. (And they will get messy.)

In a relationship with someone else, an overarching legacy of trust is created over time. Yet for years I expected myself to swoon at my own feet without first proving I could be trusted. I had expected myself to jump at each of my own requests, though I had been completely unaccountable to myself for my actions, trespasses, and many breaches of confidence. Instead of relating to and with myself, I was storming into my inner landscape, criticizing what I found there, shaming myself, and demanding changes to all my perceived inadequacies.

You may be in the same place. You may have broken your own promises or not shown up for yourself over the course of your life. Other people or institutions might not have shown up for you or have broken promises made to you. You might pull these stories out whenever you find yourself wanting to try something new, using that mountain of evidence to support your deepest suspicion that you are not worthy of kept promises. In doing so, again and again, you diminish your natural enthusiasm for whatever it was that had you excited to begin with, telling yourself the lie that you will never be capable of a trusting, fruitful, and fully embodied relationship with yourself.

This healing is relational, which means it happens IN relationship with yourself and others over your entire lifetime. You will always be in the process of navigating what it means to be the tender steward of your body and life. It became easier to see why those years of shaming myself never seemed to work for me once I began taking responsibility for the tone and quality of my self-talk. Then I was able to clearly understand the ways I best receive support and the kinds of relationships in which I have historically thrived. In my fear of never amounting to anything if I honored my own humanity, I trespassed against myself again and again. I became abusive in my attempts to force myself into action because I had been conditioned to believe that without that kind of treatment, I would never get done what I wanted to get done in my lifetime, and never live up to my potential.

At the core of this mistreatment was a supreme lack of trust. If beating myself up, formulating plan after plan for my own reinvention or trying desperately to control my very human self could work—they would have worked already.

Trust is built when you take the time to get to know yourself, support yourself, and follow through with your commitments to yourself. Trust is built when you stay by your own side even though it feels uncomfortable or you would rather run away. Trust is built knowing that even if you lose yourself along the way, you will find yourself again because you are paying attention and actively participating in your life. Trust is born from making time for yourself, even when you're busy with the details of day-to-day living, and it is cultivated when you listen to your inner wisdom and prioritize your own guidance, even if you fail. If you are going to reclaim your life and begin living in a way that is both intuitive and built on a foundation of self-responsibility, self-care, self-trust, and self-love, you are going to have to become comfortable with the idea of failure as the gathering of important data.

Trust is born in your willingness to remain by your own side. It grows with the faith that you will be there to catch yourself each and every time you fall.

Self-Love

I am cherished.

I am celebrated.

I am blooming in self-love.

Culturally, we pay lip service to the importance of self-love. Hell, every magazine rack and my Instagram feed are chock-full of it. But self-love as we've so often defined it tends to feel like a blanket we use to cover up something we don't want to look at anymore. It encourages us to say,

Oh no, that's okay! I love you anyway! through gritted teeth, even as our minds generate conflicting statements with expletives and exclamation points. Instead of being taught that even the parts of ourselves we feel are most unlovable and unholdable are indeed worthy of our kindness, we learned to distract ourselves from our disappointments by hatching plans to fix ourselves.

You are not a problem to be fixed. You are a miracle to be cherished. Feeling you are productive enough, good enough, and worthy enough is an inside job. You do not owe the world your perfection. Your pursuit of contrived goodness will never truly keep you safe because this notion of static safety is an illusion. So, once perfection and the ability to work hard to earn unconditional safety are off the table, what's left? Your truest and most fully expressed human self, living your life the best you can.

The Difference between Self-Responsibility and Hyper-Individualism

I want to make something really clear here—programmed by our culture, we tend to look at these issues through a lens of hyper-individualism. *Pull yourself up by your bootstraps! Take responsibility for your shit! Change your mindset!*

But here's the thing: whatever your stuff is, it's not your fault.

It's not your fault, but *it is your responsibility*. It's not your fault, but it is an issue that concerns your safety and well-being. It's not your fault, but it is your life. And if you want your life to feel really good, this work has to be reckoned with as lovingly and gently as possible. No one is going to be able to do this unlearning for you.

In the same turn, you are not wholly responsible for your reality. Your reality is shaped by the systems you interact with on a daily basis and specifically by the ways those systems treat you. Both are true. And what can positively impact your life is how you speak to, treat, and relate to yourself each day.

This work is complex.

Real self-love is messy and complicated. It requires space, forgiveness, and healing to flourish. This kind of love has the potential to break our hearts, as we simultaneously hold disappointment and fear with compassion and forgiveness. This kind of love may feel out of reach if you haven't had any role models teaching you how to cherish yourself this way. But it can be learned. You can teach yourself how to love and how it feels to BE loved simultaneously. This love is the active participation in your daily life and the continued choice to lean into all the glorious intricacies of your being.

You have to be willing to actively engage with your life if you want a life that feels as good on the inside as it looks from the outside. You are allowed to prioritize and honor the sacredness of your life by being discerning with your actions. You remind yourself of your innate worth each time you show up and build your capacity for living compassionately. You deliver a message in no uncertain terms each time you turn your attention toward yourself and get curious about how something feels to you and what you need to make good on your commitments.

Being alive is an extraordinary honor. When you were born, you were charged with a vast life of possibility and opportunity. One aspect of self-love includes returning to a place of awe as you relearn how to interact with your life from curiosity. We aren't guaranteed a favorable outcome just because we show up or follow through—but we do get to choose to find the joy in the process of living this way, the uniquely delicious joy of waking up each morning and choosing how we'd like to proceed.

One final note here. While the focus in this book is on *you* and *your needs*, make no mistake: this is collective work. What you're doing here is laying the groundwork for not only a new way of relating to your needs and yourself but also to others. The truth is, before you can effectively advocate for your needs with someone else, you have to be able to do so with yourself. Your first sweep through this book will have you reorganizing your life so that your needs are not only tolerated but also accepted and celebrated by *you*, as you move toward this being the baseline experience of your needs with everyone else in your life.

How to Use This Book

This isn't a book of answers. It is a book of questions, for you and about you. This book is a container, holding space for you as you begin to answer those questions for yourself.

The thoughts, prompts, and exercises in this book are invitations to return to your original energy signature as a human who requires regard, space in your schedule, and access to your time, energy, and attention to feed your own joy and curiosity—not to make you a better cog in a system that disrespects you and doesn't provide for your humanity. Throughout the following pages, I will share stories about needs. Some of those stories are my own; others belong to clients who have given me permission to share their experiences; and still others are composites of personal experiences I have encountered in conversations over the last ten years. The benedictions that begin each chapter are both my blessings to you and my vision for the fullest expression of that particular need being met. Part of my work here is modeling possibility; the blessings are equal parts modeling and experience.

If you feel you don't have time for this, know that your relationship with yourself is built through small steps and intentional daily moments. All that is required is you taking a vested interest in yourself and your needs. You don't need anything more than what you have right now—though a journal might be useful. I will share many writing prompts and questions in the coming pages. I firmly believe that getting thoughts out of the mind and onto the page brings more clarity and connection than we may have thought possible.

Things will look different on the other side of this work. You will be you, but more so. Your life will be yours, and brimming with clarity, declaration, and celebration. The life you're aching for is not only possible but also gloriously feasible. You deserve to feel at home in your skin, despite systems and forces telling you that you are not valid as you are. You have everything you need to begin making decisions that are in integrity with your values and beliefs. You can learn to live your life instead of allowing your life to live you. It is possible to practice granting yourself permission—permission to unfurl, release what no longer serves you, become, and heal the layers of hurt you've been carrying.

Tending to Your Inner Landscape

Getting to know your inner landscape is a prerequisite for tending to your needs. Your inner landscape is composed of your thoughts, feelings, self-talk, deeply held beliefs, the influence of your ancestral knowledge (including both beautiful and traumatic moments experienced by previous generations), and your personal vision for what is possible for you and your life.

One way to visually connect with your inner landscape is to imagine it as a plot of land. This plot of land has distinct boundaries, protected by a ramshackle fence that may be broken down in places or nonexistent in other places, but still this land marks a distinct space. At this moment, it might be land you don't feel very connected to or that has been unattended for a duration of time. The landscape itself might be overgrown or strewn with trash. Maybe there are vestiges from kids who had a party, with small liquor bottles littering the ground or cigarette butts between the garden beds. Maybe your inner landscape feels abandoned or desolate. Maybe you are struggling to be grateful for the ownership of such a dilapidated burden, or maybe you feel hopeful about the possibility of creating a beautiful, safe, secure, and nourishing garden. Maybe you are as ambivalent about this plot of earth as you have grown to feel about your own needs over the years. Becoming the groundskeeper of this unique swath of earth is your birthright. This landscape may be known to you, a national park with well-trodden paths and signposts, or it may be overgrown and uncultivated. This wide expanse in you is your sacred terrain whether or not you have spent much time there.

You might imagine you know yourself quite well, but you might actually be more familiar with who you want to be or believe you are expected to be than with who you actually are. You are charged with bearing witness to your own inner ecology without rushing in to fix anything. You are invited to become familiar with your patterns and ways of operating in the world, without making the presence of those inner workings mean something shameful or wrong about you. Reading this book is akin to plunking yourself down in your own wild landscape and choosing to step into your stewardship of this land.

Your first task is to familiarize yourself with the landscape by moving through it one square inch at a time and removing what does not belong to you or belong in this space. Hands deep in the dirt as you sift through the earth, your attention is on combing your expanse of land for vestiges of old conversations, stories you learned about yourself, and beliefs passed down through your family legacy—the things that don't feel right to you or don't feel right to you any longer. During your first pass over the landscape, you might remove the obvious trash or pull weeds, but as you familiarize yourself with the land, you will deepen your understanding of it and become acquainted with the complex root system beneath the growth.

As you work, you might find yourself fantasizing about what it would be like to have a more perfect plot of earth, with nutrient-rich soil and the perfect amount of sunlight, a plot of land that is more aesthetically pleasing. You might start disparaging yourself and your landscape as you compare your weeds to your view of someone else's manicured expanse of earth. Maybe if you had more money, you could hire somebody to help you or buy better tools or plants. Maybe if the conditions were different, it would be easier or better. You subtly begin abandoning your landscape, distancing yourself from its imperfections because it is painful to hold and care for them. Because it can be overwhelming to change the circumstances, how can we empower our current selves and shift our individual behaviors?

The truth is every single one of us carries triggers, tender spots, and core wounds. The belief that caring for ourselves would be easier if we had just gotten a better allotment to begin with is a belief that keeps us from the task of showing up for the bodies and lives we have. It keeps us in the place of starting again or buying into other people's systems or programs as "the fix" for our problematic humanity.

In the coming chapters, we will work with this metaphor of tending to our inner landscape because it is useful to have a visual understanding of what it means to take care of ourselves. This is active work—sweaty, with the sun beating down and hands in the dirt. Building a relationship with yourself isn't a passive process of reading an inspiring book on your lunch break. I intend to inspire you with my words, but this book is a call to action. Beginning to tend to your inner landscape is about allowing your needs to exist, to be exactly what they are—inconvenient, ridiculous, frustrating, and brilliant. It is the practice of allowing your needs to be welcomed even when you do not have the means to fulfill them at this exact moment.

The Sweet Spot Between Patience and Avoidance

This process is, well, just that—a process. It's not linear, and it looks different for every person every day. Be patient with yourself as you go through it. And keep an eye out for potential avoidance.

You might find it complicated to start this process of stewardship. That's okay. It's not a race. That being said, you do yourself a disservice if you put this process off indefinitely. Only you can know if you're procrastinating or not. You are the expert of your own experience. You determine the pace. Having confidence in your inner knowing and reporting your needs are facets of self-trust.

The trickiest part about beginning this work after a lifetime of striving and bullying yourself into greater and greater levels of productivity is navigating your way into the cozy spot between hiding from yourself and sabotaging your new and slow path to care. It takes time to soften into moving at your own pace. Having patience with yourself as you hone your way to this sweet spot is crucial, because divesting from the toxic productivity of our culture is an unlearning process.

Journal prompts to dive deeper:

How do I feel about how I am showing up for myself right now?

If I'm really honest, have I been caring for myself in the way I most wish to be cared for?

If not, why?

Where am I hiding out because it's hard, because I resist, or because I struggle with how to follow through with what I said I would do?

Here's what I know—you DO know the answers to these questions. You just have to practice asking them of yourself. Daily tending is an intentionally permissive and expansive process. I am actively encouraging you to move at your own pace, while also lovingly holding you accountable for the reason you picked up this book. You joined me here because you needed a new way to approach your life. Whatever brought you here, hold on to that desire for yourself and your life as you practice. You're in charge here. You're sovereign in your actions. You get to choose. And you're learning to hold yourself accountable with kindness, curiosity, and love.

Practice: Your Daily Check-In

A practice is an opportunity to follow through with small acts to rebuild self-trust. A practice is meant to be exactly that, something you work on and toward instead of waiting until you can do it perfectly or have all of the correct tools or feel ready to begin. The practices in this book are opportunities to show up for yourself in different ways, doing the best you can. You're under no obligation to do this perfectly, though you're invited to do this with as much delicious consistency as you can muster.

This first practice, the daily check-in, is at the core of figuring out what you need and how to care for yourself each and every day. I highly recommend doing this in the morning, but, as with all things in *Needy*, please tailor this practice for your use.

And as you're easing into your daily check-in, know that at first you do not have to DO anything with the data you're collecting if you do not feel ready. This practice is about following your breath into your body and taking five minutes out of your day to check in with yourself and how you're feeling.

Close your eyes and feel your feet on the floor. Take a few deep breaths with your hands on your heart or your belly.

When you feel ready, ask yourself:

How do I feel?

What do I need?

What does my body need from me?

What is ONE need I am ready, able, and willing to meet today?

As you open your eyes, make a plan with yourself about how and when you will meet the one need that showed up during your check-in. Put it on your calendar. Ask a friend to hold you accountable. Devote yourself to yourself by whatever means necessary. Commit to showing up as best you can as you carve out space for your needs. Keep it simple. And follow through.

Please Get It Wrong

As you move through this practice and into the following pages, give yourself permission to skip around. Or to read straight through. Share an important passage with a friend. Ask for help. Do it "wrong."

You do not have to do this (or anything) perfectly. Truly. Doing the work in this book is an invitation to self-trust, because let me be clear: you will get it "wrong." You may lose your way. You build trust when you find your way back to yourself again. You can use the tools in this book to bring yourself back to where you want to be—which feels so much better than shaming yourself and making yourself "bad" for doing the work in this book the "wrong" way.

Let's just agree right here and right now that life happens and that you will respond to whatever comes up as it comes up with compassion and trust (even if it's only a tentative trust right now.)

Move at your own pace, but hold yourself accountable to what you started when you picked up this book—crafting a life for yourself that puts YOU at the center. When I say YOU, I am speaking specifically to your dreams, needs, deep desires, strange quirks, peculiarities, and creative ways of doing things. There is room for all of it in your life, I promise, and you will feel better for it.

This work is not a bootcamp or a glossy plan for reinvention. It is a conversation to have with yourself as you navigate your daily life. I will never urge you to aspire to platinum-level self-love or shame you for doing this work too slowly. In fact, I encourage you to do less. I encourage you to lose your way so that you can practice finding yourself again. I encourage you to opt out of anything here that doesn't feel deliciously doable.

This work is cyclical. Iterative. It is how you learn to know, care for, trust, and love yourself, instead of waiting for some magical love epiphany to bop you on the head and make ALL of this easier. Part of what makes this framework inevitable is the self-admiration you acquire alongside the radical self-responsibility of being willing to muck through it all for and with yourself—proving to yourself that you are worthy of the kind of deep care, commitment, and reverence you hunger for. Throughout this book, I'll show you how each of the four stages applies in the main foundational areas that make up our lives, giving you a chance to dance between the stages as you learn to take up space in your own life with confidence and grace.

CHAPTER 2

Safety

You exist. You're real. You're a human being with needs, desires, and dreams. Your inner spark is inextinguishable—no matter how deeply your light feels buried in this moment.

You matter.

Your needs matter. The presence of your needs is a fact of your humanity and not a moral failing or flaw revealing your inadequacy.

Your experience of your life matters.

This is an invitation and invocation for your most essential, tender, and true self. The one buried beneath the many roles you play each day. The one pushed aside in frustration when a need presents itself at an inconvenient time. The part of you that knows exactly who you are and what you require to thrive.

How do you support yourself in feeling safe?

How do you tend to your inner child, hungry to be seen, held, and nourished?

How do you create systems and structures of self-support that you may have never experienced in your relationships before?

How do you purposefully create moments of grounding in an ungrounded world?

How do you become a leader in your own inner landscape, calming the chaos and taking responsibility for your upkeep?

Layer by layer. Tender, inspired action after tender, inspired action.

There is no right place to start, so start where you're standing. It's the perfect place, I promise.

"IT WAS A DARK AND STORMY NIGHT." Madeleine L'Engle's strong, slightly raspy voice boomed through my bedroom in the dark, dampening the bullying voices echoing in my head.

I listened to *A Wrinkle in Time* on repeat my whole sixth-grade year—it was the only thing that lulled me into feeling safe enough to fall asleep at night, when my mind wouldn't stop churning over every moment of rejection and cruelty I'd encountered that day.

She's so needy.

She actually thinks she's pretty.

Her parents are divorced. They fight all the time.

She believes in all of that weird stuff about crystals and energy healing.

She thinks she's SO smart.

She's fat.

She's disgusting.

Did you see what she was wearing? I KNOW. It's so embarrassing!

One morning in December of that year, I had become an outcast overnight after my childhood best friend spread lies about me to the other girls in the class, turning them all against me. When I arrived at school that day, no one would speak to me, and it was weeks before I truly understood why. Bit by bit, the stories about what I'd allegedly said were revealed. It wasn't just these lies that were spread. It was the inner-most details of the bright, shiny light of my sixth-grade confidence—the things I was wondering about and the meaning I was beginning to make of the world and my place in it.

After that morning, I would lie awake at night, anxiously churning through everything I had said during the day—and everything that was said to and about me. I poured myself into inspecting myself for flaws and making plans to make myself impenetrable to criticism.

I will make myself likable. Inoffensive. Pretty and smart, but not threatening. Someone whom everyone wants to be around, but no one envies. Someone palatable. Someone easy.

I will make myself indisputably average.

I will belong.

I will keep myself safe.

I carry the pain and confusion of those months with me. Those relationships were important to me at such a vital time in my social upbringing and the loss of them shattered my sense of being secure in a community of women. Not only did it not feel safe to be myself, it also felt treacherous to like myself as I was. It was heartbreaking to be bullied this way and ultimately taught me to be self-protective and perfectionistic in my relationships because I feared it might happen again. It was almost twenty years before I rebuilt the necessary self-trust and love to feel resilient enough to risk bringing my true, most real, and fully expressed self to a friendship again.

Safety hinged to perfectionism is not true safety. It is the white-knuckle plan of the heartbroken and rejected, resolute in their desire to protect themselves from future abandonment. This false safety followed me through my life until I realized that it isolated me in my panic for external validation and acceptance.

In an effort to belong to others, I had stopped belonging to myself.

Perhaps you relate. Perhaps you, too, could never cover yourself up adequately, living in fear of the moment when your imperfect self would spill out over the edges, touching everything around you, bubbling up out of your core. And no matter how much you tried, you just felt more alone—and more unsafe.

Journal prompts to dive deeper:

What does the idea of safety bring up for you?

What are some physical, behavioral, or emotional signs that you feel safe?

What are some physical, behavioral, or emotional signs that you do not feel safe?

What memories do you carry of moments when you felt the safest?

What memories do you carry of moments when you didn't feel safe?

What conditions do you require for your need for safety to be met?

Meeting Your Need for Safety

Safety is an individual and collective need. Physical safety includes the absence of harm to our bodies, access to water and food, shelter, and a baseline of reliably meeting our financial needs. Emotional safety hinges on our experience of positive regard, well-being, and the absence of emotional harm in our relationships. Our emotional safety also includes our experience of our own inner landscape—the self-talk and beliefs that are the foundation of our relationship with ourselves.

Having our need for safety met doesn't necessarily indicate the absence of threat. Instead, safety can come from a rooted sense of being connected to yourself and to the world around you in meaningful ways. This distinction can be powerful for those of us who have experienced or are experiencing threats as we navigate our daily lives. It offers us an opportunity to experiment with aspects of tending to our need for safety now, even if we still feel unsafe in other aspects of our lives.

Much of this chapter will focus on cultivating safety in your relationship with yourself, but it would be a mistake not to begin with the very real ways that systemic violence, oppression, and an unequal division of resources impact our need for safety. This violence and trauma are passed down through lineages and spread through family lines, braided into every facet of our lived experience and defining our energetic capacity. Prioritizing your needs, pleasure, thriving, and joy may be more challenging depending on your access, but *that doesn't make them any less vital for you*. You're a human. You have needs. One of those needs is safety.

Your need for safety is your energetic tether to the earth below you. Beyond having your basic safety needs met, "feeling safe" is relative. You're more likely to feel grounded when you navigate your life with an awareness of your inner landscape, an understanding of your social conditioning, and a firmly held desire to stay by your own side no matter what life presents. You're more likely to feel rooted when you're seen, heard, known, and held—skills you can practice in your relationship with yourself and then with your chosen community. When your primary need for safety is met, you're more energetically available to meet your other needs. If your most basic safety needs go unmet, it can be much more taxing to contribute to the world in meaningful ways or to celebrate or express yourself fully.

Attending to your need for safety requires you to look at both your immediate, day-to-day needs and your longer-term needs. Though we all share an overarching need for safety, we each have things we specifically and personally require to feel safe, things other people might not even think about. This requires you to take the time to get to know yourself so that you can take better care of yourself, while caring for yourself so that you also have the energetic capacity to foster that relationship. It asks you to take radical responsibility for your needs before you understand them fully, and certainly before you've unlearned the conditioning that tells us we don't deserve access to our own attention. This was certainly the case for Ava,

Ava was married to a loud, affectionate man whom she loved deeply. But whenever the two would get into an argument, he was verbose and quick on his feet while Ava was overwhelmed and at a loss for words. Recalling her intense fear that her father would leave whenever her parents fought during her childhood, Ava felt flooded by the volume of her husband's voice in their conversations and the quickness with which he was able to speak his mind. Taken back to those moments in childhood, Ava understood that she was afraid her husband might leave her if she didn't acquiesce or agree with him, and over time she'd retreated further into herself, always stunned in the face of conflict and unable to figure out what she wanted to say fast enough. Then it always seemed the moment had passed, and she figured, *why bother*.

Ava had multiple safety needs in these moments—the need to ask for a break to collect herself when overwhelmed in this way, tools to regulate her nervous system during moments of conflict, and a way to reconnect with her husband after the fact to continue the conversation and express herself. The act of identifying these needs in and of themselves felt huge to Ava— but as she practiced sharing her needs ahead of time, with a predetermined plan in place, she began to feel safer navigating these conversations. With time, she was even able to create a plan with her husband for how they would have difficult discussions together—how they would pause if she felt overwhelmed and allow for whatever she needed in those moments, which might be space to herself, a shower, a walk outside, and how once she felt calmer, they'd pick up the conversation again, or if it still felt scary for Ava, they'd have the conversation in writing over email or text.

Over the course of your life, have you felt seen, held, and positively regarded? Or did your feelings and needs seem to overwhelm or upset your grown-ups? Much of this conditioning is rooted in formative experiences of how our needs were met during childhood, as well as examples of care we witnessed directly and indirectly.

In adulthood, we're offered an opportunity to explore this conditioning and to reparent ourselves by providing for our physical, emotional, mental, energetic, and spiritual needs on a daily basis. Cultivating safety and grounding in your relationship with yourself is essential for creating a solid foundation for the rest of your life. It is rooted in consistently attending to your basic needs for water, shelter, and food, as well as making a vested effort to be intentional with your meaning-making and self-talk. It's not about working ON yourself; it's about working WITH yourself. It's about being present and curious about what is going on in your body (needs) and mind (inner landscape).

Let's begin by bringing a sense of awareness and stewardship to your inner landscape.

Imagine your thoughts are like a wild crew of children on a playground, running in every direction. In this scenario, you're the teacher on playground duty. It's your job to kindly tend to this herd of children.

As they run around all over the place, inevitably one of them ends up eating sand or pulling things out of the trashcan or doing some other unsavory thing, and as the teacher, it's your job to redirect them as kindly as possible. (Even if it's for the millionth time and through gritted teeth, which is totally okay. You're human after all.)

This scenario is wonderful because it reminds you to use your kindest language as you redirect yourself. You would not tell a child they were a stupid failure for making a mistake or mock them mercilessly for believing they weren't good enough (again). Stepping into our role as the tender steward of our inner landscape and the sovereign leader of our thoughts takes a bit of discipline. Tending isn't the absence of discipline. It's the gift of discipline delivered with unconditional love.

Journal prompts to dive deeper:

What thoughts or feelings come up for you when you think about keeping yourself safe?

When in your life have you felt most seen, heard, and held?

What systems of oppression impact your experience of safety on a daily basis?

What grief do you carry around experiences of safety or a lack thereof?

What is a ritual or routine you could create to support yourself in feeling more safe and grounded each day?

 ### Practice: Befriending Your Inner Child

You were born to the world in an instant. In the best-case scenario, you instantly exited the warm comfort of your parent's womb, where you had been sheltered and cared for by their body with delicious consistency. You went from being connected to being an autonomous human being with needs. You began a new kind of dependency, one that relied on your ability to use the rudimentary skills you'd been granted to indicate to the world around you that you were in need of attention.

In the first moments of my daughter's life, I was exhausted. Having been in labor for fifty-six hours, all I wanted to do was sleep. I'd lost her twin in the first trimester and had already been battling with postpartum depression for much of my pregnancy, which was only compounded after Delphina's birth as I struggled to learn how to care for her when I felt I needed so much care myself.

In the days following her long and challenging birth, I became obsessed with how we go from being nourished and tended to, to having to advocate for our needs using the rudimentary newborn skills available to us. In that moment, we are born into a world full of systems that categorize our worth by the color of our skin, gender identity, socioeconomic class, sexual identity, and abilities. Our ancestors were directly impacted by those systems, and we are also inadvertently impacted by them from the moment of conception.

How do we begin to explore the deeply held beliefs and memories we shoulder about what it has meant to be needy in a world that is not built for us to nourish ourselves?

How do we reparent ourselves in a world full of systems that exploit and oppress us based on identities beyond our control?

How do we tend to the wounds we carry about what it means to be a human with needs—even when those around us are unwilling or unavailable to meet those needs?

It's impossible to cultivate a solid and grounded relationship with ourselves without walking our way back to our first days, when we began receiving messages about our too-muchness, neediness, or the conflict between having needs and needing to belong to our families of origin. It's important to begin here because the moment of your birth is the instant you began learning what it meant to ask, to feel hindered by not having the language or skills to advocate for yourself, and to attach the value of your needs to the response you received when you made them known. The purpose of walking back to your beginning days is not to persecute your caregivers, but instead to gather up compassion for yourself as you learn how and why you've withdrawn so that you can begin the repair of coaxing your signals out of hiding.

You had needs. You have needs now. You're allowed to have needs. You're allowed to have needs no matter how your needs are received by the humans around you. You're allowed to advocate for your needs whether or not the humans in your life have the bandwidth to join you in meeting your needs. The worth and value of your needs are not correlated to whether or not someone else has the bandwidth for them.

Your neediness is a fact. Your worth is inherent. Your value is indisputable.

Making the daily choice to care for yourself and not to abandon yourself no matter how unwieldy or uncomfortable your needs are is how you set things right. In doing so, you repair your understanding about what it means to have your needs met in your primary relationship. However, if you move directly to asking yourself what you need, you skip the vital step of practicing how you speak to yourself. The tone of your self-talk can dictate a feeling of safety and openness in your inner landscape, but so many of us are accustomed to speaking to ourselves critically or even cruelly when no one is looking.

START HERE

Find a photo of yourself as a baby or a young child and put it front and center on your altar, desk, or anywhere you pass by often. If you do not have a photo of yourself at an early age, you could draw one or choose the youngest photo you have available.

Begin using this photo of your child-self as a litmus test for your self-talk.

Would I say this to myself as a child? Is this how I would treat myself if I were a baby entrusted to my care?

Let that guide you, and please note that if your answer no, such treatment is not good enough for you either. Let your child-self guide you as you refocus and begin teaching yourself how to be unendingly gentle.

THIS MIGHT LOOK LIKE . . .

If you're at the self-responsibility stage, this might look like an acknowledgement that your needs exist. Maybe you tend to them. Maybe you don't. If nothing else, you might stop being so harsh with yourself.

If you're at the self-care stage, this might look like an increased responsiveness and kindness to yourself. You lose the judgment of your needs and start showing yourself (past and present) that you're able and willing to meet them.

If you're at the self-trust stage, this might look like the formation of a positive feedback loop. You've shown yourself you can and will respond to your needs, and you start caring for "now-you" with the same softness and love you would give the "then-you." You may even start anticipating your needs or building habits to meet them.

If you're at the self-love stage, this might look like a deepening into the relationship and care you've already cultivated. You may develop an increased sensitivity to your needs or start to understand nuances in them you didn't know before.

If you're at the advocacy stage, this might look like noticing the people in your life who speak to you in a way that feels harmful to your inner child and deciding whether that is a person you want to continue having a relationship with. If so, begin thinking about having a conversation with them about how their words impact you.

Wherever you are in this process, connecting daily with your younger self is a powerful reminder that you still require the connection and care you ache for. Being an adult does not invalidate those needs. Allow your younger self to urge you toward giving yourself more self-compassion and kindness each day.

What It Means to Take Radical Responsibility for Your Life

The other side of safety is trusting in your bones that you are willing to take responsibility for yourself and your life—particularly if you have a history of self-abandonment in times of difficulty, failure, or disappointment or when you risk being rejected. Our need for safety goes unmet when we continue well-worn patterns and behaviors of self-abandonment.

How do you speak to yourself when a project goes sideways or you feel disappointed in yourself? Does your self-talk replicate the urgency, perfectionism, and forced productivity that exist in the world around you? Do you have a tendency to abandon yourself before you can be rejected by others? Do you routinely bypass your unique brilliance and way of going about things and instead pursue one-size-fits-all solutions? Do you seek and prioritize external validation or feedback over your own felt sense of enoughness? These are examples of how you might undermine your need for safety in your relationship with yourself each day. These incidents might seem small in and of themselves, but with time they pile up on one another, forming a mountain of evidence that shows you cannot and will not keep yourself safe when met with an obstacle or discomfort. They are examples of you turning away from yourself when it counts instead of turning toward yourself with curiosity and compassion.

We meet our need for safety when we refuse to leave our own side no matter what happens, thereby ensuring that even when times are challenging we are willing to meet ourselves in the muck of it and work to figure it out. Cultivating this type of steadfast relationship with yourself requires practice, patience, and self-compassion, as you expand your tolerance for discomfort and unlearn patterns of self-abandonment. This doesn't mean you think you are perfect or you don't have areas in your life to work on. It does mean you have a vested interest in approaching your life from your own side as you figure out what comes next. Taking responsibility for our lives, our needs, and our wants means we are willing to remain in conversation with ourselves regardless of the noise from external feedback. This responsibility is the opposite of forced perfectionism or earning our own care by jumping through hoops to deserve it. Instead, it is rooted in the resolute knowing that we are humans doing the best we can and that by relating to ourselves from a place of grounded safety, we can create change in our own lives and the world around us.

Of course, this work first requires you to understand that you are in a relationship with yourself and that relationship is valuable to your felt experience of safety and overall satisfaction. Explicitly connecting with yourself and tending to your relationship with yourself may be a new concept for you, but there's nothing more important. After all, your relationship with yourself is the only relationship that spans the entirety of your life.

It might feel a little funny to play both parts in this relationship, like childhood games where you spoke your words aloud while making your animals, dolls, or trucks talk back to you. To begin tending to yourself with confidence and compassion, you need to remember (and accept) that you're both the asker and the provider. You're the vulnerable and the strong. You're the needy child and the loving parent.

Taking responsibility for yourself begins as a dialogue between these parts. When you turn your attention to your body by considering how you feel and understanding your needs, you're offered a chance to reconnect with a part of yourself you may have lost contact with or even never felt associated with. You will receive opportunities to care for yourself with patience and perseverance in both tangible and intangible ways.

It's likely you disconnected from parts of yourself for many valid reasons. Maybe you experienced trauma, which has made it complicated and painful to exist in your body. Maybe you were raised in a family where your needs weren't allowed, honored, or well tended. Maybe the daily rigor of capitalism, patriarchy, and White supremacy taught you that your worth is rooted in what you do and produce for others, instead of in your humanity and inherent wholeness.

Maybe, just maybe, you've been doing the best you can with what you've had to work with. I think it's important to start here, in deep reverence of your having done whatever you needed to make it to this point.

Before you read on, take a moment to put your hand on your heart. Thank yourself for everything you did to keep yourself safe in the past. Thank yourself for everything you're doing at this current moment to support yourself to the best of your abilities. Thank yourself for everything you will do from this moment forward to take responsibility for your body, your needs, and your life.

The cardinal rule in rebuilding a safe and trustworthy relationship with yourself is patience with the process. It might take time to regain your own trust. Your needs might take you in directions that are inconvenient or uncomfortable. This isn't about perfection or even taking action. Instead, we rebuild trust when we reclaim our inner landscape by attending to how we speak to ourselves *about* our choices. These internal negotiations and deeply felt understandings make all the difference. Be gentle with yourself as you explore here. You deserve the utmost care and kindness. And remember, all of this is a practice, which means you will get it wrong as often as you get it right.

Tending to Yourself Is an Act of Rebuilding Trust

Radical self-responsibility informs self-care and rebuilds self-trust. This trust meets your need for safety as you recognize you have decided to matter to yourself. When you take inspired action, you don't take your gifts for granted or trespass against your needs. You won't leave your body behind to produce unsustainably. You endeavor to remain by your own side, even with a history of self-abandonment. You value yourself for everything that you ARE—which exists alongside everything you are not or are not yet.

You keep what you value safe. You place what you value in safety deposit boxes or files marked important, and you make sure not to misplace or ruin what you hold dear to your heart. You devote yourself to tending to what you value. You detail your car, polish your silver, and make sure not to spill your coffee onto your computer. If you're to keep yourself safe, you must decide you're valuable and worthy of your own safekeeping and then rebuild self-trust with that decision.

Self-trust is generated through a simple principle: follow through. When you don't do what you've said you were going to do, don't abandon yourself. Instead, get curious about what happened and work WITH yourself. This approach might be radically different from what you've experienced before, but it is possible to hold yourself accountable in a kind way. Maybe you struggle to follow through with your commitments, and your negative self-talk is rooted in the belief that you will fail again, as you always have. Follow-through might not be your issue, but you may still act in ways that are unnecessarily cruel, unsustainable, and damaging to your sense of self-trust. In either scenario, the way you relate to yourself impacts the totality of your experience and can damage your understanding of who you are and what is possible for you.

There are many legitimate reasons why you might struggle with following through for yourself, and I promise we will explore some of these reasons in more detail in the coming chapters. However, to begin rebuilding your self-trust and cultivate a feeling of safety and security in your relationship with yourself sooner rather than later, I am asking you not to wait until you've got it all figured out to begin trying to follow through. Traditional self-help culture might have you working to get to the bottom of the original hurt, but you do not need to know why you do the things you do to start doing them differently.

There is no guaranteed intellectual exercise or depth of self-knowledge that is going to get you to stand up, walk over to the faucet, fill your cup, and drink it multiple times a day. Your lack of hydration is indicative of a larger trend in your life, AND it's the simple need to slow yourself down enough to make sure you remember to refill your cup.

This week, devote yourself to follow-through by using your daily check-in practice as consistently as possible. Use whatever tools you need to remind yourself of this intention. Use a chart and stickers or bribe yourself with something fabulous if you must. Write yourself a million notes. Devote yourself to yourself, imperfectly, and know that you're rebuilding your self-trust each time you show up.

Journal prompts to dive deeper:

Take a moment to tune in to the quality of your self-talk on a regular day. Would you feel safe in a relationship with someone if they spoke to you that same way?

How do you speak to yourself when you think about starting something new?

How do you speak to yourself when you've disappointed yourself or made a mistake?

What thoughts pass through your mind when someone pays you a compliment?

How does it feel to slow down and focus on the quality and content of your self-talk?

Practice: Tending to Your Discomfort

It's possible you've gotten to this part of the book and are already ready to be done. You might be feeling the pain of years of unmet safety needs, the grief of not feeling safe with others or yourself for so long. This pain is real, and it matters. And there's more to be had here. Feeling uncomfortable does not mean you are doing this work incorrectly or should wait for a better time to begin. It does mean there is a part of you showing up to be seen and heard, and most importantly, that you get to choose how to care for yourself in whatever way feels most doable in the moment.

Tending to your discomfort is an essential practice for deepening into identifying, honoring, and advocating for your needs because it opens the door to the presence of your feelings during the process. It can be painful to start setting boundaries at work or with loved ones. It can be intimidating to say something aloud that you believe the other person might not be available to receive. It can feel overwhelming to open the door to your needs only to become fully present to an onslaught of unmet needs from years past. And yet, on the other side of that discomfort lives a world of full self-expression, satisfied needs, and right-sized relationships.

As the saying goes, the only way forward is through. But you do not need to muscle through your discomfort without caring for your physical, emotional, mental, and spiritual needs. Between the polar opposites of making your needs and desires wrong because they are uncomfortable and bearing down and barreling through them is a vast field of nuance and tending. Cultivating ways to stand by your own side during times of discomfort and strong emotion is infinitely useful, regardless of the circumstance that gave rise to the challenging feeling.

START HERE

Whenever you get caught up in a strong emotion, pause and ask yourself:

What am I feeling right now?

What supports me when I feel this way?

How can I hold space for my feelings and care for myself in this moment?

Instead of stopping, experiment with tending to *that* need.

THIS MIGHT LOOK LIKE ...

If you're at the self-responsibility stage, this might look like noticing and verbalizing your discomfort. Say out loud, "I feel uncomfortable right now. What do I need?" to remind yourself that feeling uncomfortable doesn't indicate anything wrong with feeling the way you feel.

If you're at the self-care stage, this might look like wrapping yourself in a blanket, phoning a friend, writing in your journal, or pouring yourself into whatever feels best in the moment.

If you're at the self-trust stage, this might look like anticipating discomfort whenever you are at the precipice of something new. There is something deeply comforting about being met in this way, as if all your feelings are right on schedule and there is nothing to be alarmed by.

If you're at the self-love stage, this might look like having a menu of go-to items for even the tiniest sign of distress or discomfort. These well-used tools are guaranteed to support you in feeling held and whole in no time.

If you're at the advocacy stage, this might look like incorporating these tools in your relationships with others so that they know how to support you during moments of distress or discomfort. For example, as Eleanor did the work of learning what she needed when she was upset, she found she was then able to ask her sister to meet her in those needs by explicitly asking for what she wanted—a hug or getting under a cozy blanket with her to watch a favorite movie. Opening herself up to receive support not only helped Eleanor meet her need for safety but also formed a bond of greater intimacy between Eleanor and her sister.

Choose to meet yourself in your discomfort. Choose to work with yourself instead of against yourself. Cultivate an environment of safety so that you feel comfortable experimenting and trying new things, even in moments of fear or overwhelm. This choice is an act of kindness and devotion that'll see you through to the other side. Developing a relationship with yourself means learning how to operate out of care for yourself, using all the data you've accumulated about yourself in action over the course of your life.

With time and practice, your feelings and needs will become more familiar to you. You will start to craft lists of remedies for specific aches and lovingly administer them for yourself when needed. Maybe when you feel uncomfortable, you need to be physically held or understood in a conversation with someone; maybe you need to understand yourself better through journal writing or to nourish yourself with your favorite comfort foods. Maybe you'll find it's time for a nap, or to listen to your favorite audiobook, or to fill the tub. There is no one right way to tend to your discomfort. This exploration is meant to be turned over to you and your needs.

Cultivating Safety in the Face of Fear and Uncertainty

Pain, suffering, systemic oppression, and profound uncertainty exist in the world around us, and it can be easy to underestimate small acts of grounding in meeting our need for safety. It can feel as though each effort is but one small drop in an enormous bucket, which cannot undo a lifetime of personal experience, trauma, or centuries of injustice. What if we stopped thinking about meeting our need for safety as rectifying a lifetime of feeling unsafe and instead started to get curious about what we require to feel seen, heard, and held by ourselves and in this moment? What feelings would we permit? What tending might those feelings inspire? How might it feel to be met this way day in and day out? What sort of trust would that build? Would we experience that trust as a deep faith in being held in our relationship with ourselves over time? The tools offered here for meeting your need for safety are vital to each of us as we learn to meet that fear and uncertainty as rooted and resourced as possible. Learning how to heal a history of self-abandonment by partnering with yourself will enable you to bring more of your vitality and self-expression to your relationships because you will be grounded in your relationship with yourself first and foremost.

Commitments to My Need for Safety

— I exist, and I have real needs. Safety—individual and collective—is one of them. I start with safety because my bandwidth for everything else will be less until this need is met.

— While I am primarily focusing on my needs in my relationship with myself, it's impossible to ignore the bigger cultural context of my lineage and where I live. It has real impacts on my life and my needs. No matter what challenges it poses for me, I still deserve justice and safety.

— Attending to my need for safety includes focusing on both my immediate day-to-day needs and taking inspired action in the direction of my longer-term aims. To do this, I have to take the time to get to know myself and foster my energetic capacity to remain by my own side.

— How do I cultivate these things? By attending to and stewarding my inner landscape. This includes seeing what is without judgment, building trust with myself by following through on meeting my needs, and cultivating the conditions I require to feel safe in my relationship with myself.

CHAPTER 3

Rest

BLESSING

Start getting ready for sleep before you feel ready for sleep.

Turn your attention to yourself and plainly say, "You're enough. You have done enough."

Put down your devices. Forgive the part of your spirit that wants to buck against your deep exhaustion and keep you awake, vigilant and yearning. Remind yourself that the validation you ache for is an inside job and resist the urge to do "just one more thing."

As you brush your teeth and wash your face, look at yourself in the mirror. Thank every gray hair. Every wrinkle. Every dark circle. Bless the energy you have expended today and turn your attention to receiving the rest you long for.

With each step, affirm your deserving and soften into receiving your own care. Tell yourself, "I am so proud of you."

No, rest won't feel comfortable at first. No, you won't feel as though you deserve it. No, it isn't much fun. No, you can't go without it just this once.

Climb into bed. Remind yourself that getting into bed is not a punishment. If you feel tense, remind yourself that you don't have to go to sleep yet. Read, gaze blankly at the wall while deep in thought, watch a TV show, or intimately connect with yourself or someone else.

As you wind down, imagine you're walking a path home to your body. As you get closer, envision yourself as a house with the glow of soft lighting in the windows and the warmth of a roaring fire in the living room. Imagine walking through your own front door and curling up in the safety of your own arms. Take comfort in how good it feels to surrender any belief that you should be doing anything other than enjoying your own company before drifting off to sleep.

I AM A TO-DO LIST MAKER AND SAVER. I relish flipping through vestiges of lists from past weeks and remembering the different things I prioritized at the time. At one point, however, I flipped through a handful of to-do lists and realized that the spot I had carved out for moving my body was left almost entirely unattended, for *fifty weeks!*

If I'm really honest with myself, I resisted the awkward muckiness of starting a new routine after an injury. I bought into the idea that there would be a better time, a time when things were less shitty and strained. My perfectionism wanted movement to look like something my body wasn't currently capable of, and this caused me to feel like a failure every time I approached it. I had fallen into the trap of feeling I should perfectly anticipate all my needs and then schedule them in neat and tidy blocks so that I wouldn't drop any of the pieces or let anyone down. But that's just not possible.

This is where we find the culture of toxic productivity that is rooted in perfectionism and capitalism—where *tomorrow* or next month or next year will be better to begin instead of today. This is where you have been conditioned to put your needs off until a more convenient time because your worth is defined by how much you produce. Toxic productivity culture is also part of diet culture, where every time you stray from your diet, you declare a fresh start, as you were taught, and recommit to your goal instead of honoring your needs as they wax and wane.

The truth is that there is no time that is better, less messy, or easier to begin. Instead of waiting for this magical, nonexistent time, this is an invitation to hold your own hand as you wade through the discomfort of being new at something. Instead of looking to perfectionism for gold stars and beautifully landscaped paths from here to there, I invite you to break your desired actions down into smaller and smaller goals until they no longer intimidate you into inaction. Sure, you will be forced to reckon with the judgmental voice in your head that says *THAT IS NOT ENOUGH TO BE WORTH YOUR TIME.* But I raise you those fifty weeks—fifty weeks of not doing a damn thing because I wasn't ready, able, or willing to grapple with my own expectations of what was "worth" doing.

It isn't lost on me that during that time, I missed out on fifty solid weeks of deliciously imperfect action, of doing less more often, and meeting myself where I was instead of bullying myself for not being where I thought I should be. I invite you to think about how this applies not only to movement or habit-building but also to the one thing we know we all need yet put off the most—rest.

Meeting Your Need for Rest

Give yourself the permission you need right now to rest. Even if that feels impossible. Even if you don't yet know how. You only need to peek outside your door to see that rest is a necessary part of the cycle of life taking place in the natural world. You have permission to rest the same way morning glories close at dusk. The same way the tide ebbs and flows, and the same way the bears hibernate in winter. Tending to your need for rest is not a sign of weakness but of how you lovingly care for your own weariness, patching yourself up where you have worn thin.

The tricky part about all of this is that you *can* borrow against your energetic resources for a certain period of time, giving you the unsustainable illusion that you can keep doing so forever. Your energy is finite, and if you continue to muscle through and deny your need for rest, you will reach a point of feeling so burned-out your body will cry out for your attention in louder and louder ways until you're forced to pay attention.

You might be weary from a lifetime of holding yourself together, looking over your shoulder to make sure your frayed ends aren't trailing behind you when you leave the house each morning. You might feel weary from the dance of self-sabotage each time you feel yourself gathering too much steam or taking up too much space. You might feel weary as you think about the promises you haven't kept to yourself and the ways you haven't had your own back over the years. Perhaps your need for rest has changed as you've grown older or experienced hormonal shifts, and you've grown weary from pretending this isn't true while keeping pace with the expectations of your younger self.

No matter where it comes from, your weariness is indisputable and valid. Being a human in the twenty-first century is exhausting. Our daily lives are riddled with loud noises, bright shiny things demanding our attention, expectations that exceed our individual capacities, and structural oppression that unequally impacts those of us with historically marginalized identities. Capitalism requires productivity at any cost—even when that cost is the quality of life for the humans operating within it. Your weariness is not only indisputable and valid but also the inevitable by-product of a world that prioritizes doing over being. This is why we are more comfortable engaging in self-care practices that somehow make us better and prioritize our tending only when the returns on our efforts are socially approved. Although rest will make you more productive, patient, and resilient in the long run, rest is also agitating because the person who will benefit most from your rest is **you**. Rest is still yours for the taking. It isn't possible for the sun to shine twenty-four hours a day, 365 days a year. Neither can you sustain a breakneck pace of production and creation—not because there is something wrong with you but because you're human.

But . . . but . . . but . . . what about productivity?

What about getting stuff done? What about the things you want to do more than rest? We have been conditioned to believe anything that takes us away from our productivity is a threat to our worthiness. We have been taught that rest is something to be earned by hard work and good behavior. Simultaneously, we have been conditioned to believe that the job will never be done well enough for us to rest. Operating within this system, there is little wonder why you're in endless pursuit of productivity, judge your need for rest, and why your need for rest always seems to compete with the things that bring you joy—your productive hours never come into question.

In your mind's eye, bring yourself back to your inner landscape and imagine sitting down on the earth. Meeting your need for rest isn't about the actions of self-responsibility we spoke about before—weeding, recycling old cans or scrap metal, or tilling the soil. Rest requires a different kind of responsibility. Meeting your need for rest is about slowing down and bringing your attention to the subtle needs of your body. This quiet solitude is necessary to begin collecting data about who and how you are at any given moment. As you give yourself permission to slow down, you get to know yourself so that you can take better care of yourself.

Before resting, your inner landscape might feel chaotic and fraught. You might be tending to the land with a looming crisis just out of view—a storm system you have to safeguard yourself against. Your actions might be swift and fueled by adrenaline. Prioritizing rest is akin to settling down on the earth in the eye of a storm, where the sun is shining and the air is still. It's about enjoying your connection to the earth first, without rushing to change or improve upon it. Instead of struggling under the belief that you have to DO anything with this plot of earth, time in rest is spent in relationship with the land, running your hand over the soil and singing to each new weed you encounter. The relationship doesn't feel forced or rushed. It's luxurious to be with yourself this way, slowly and steady, as if you have an entire lifetime of connection ahead of you. You do.

As you pursue bringing more rest into your life, you might notice that your doing so agitates the people around you. Giving yourself permission to rest might change the way you show up in your relationships. You might begin to create boundaries where there were none. You might trigger people in your life as your softening illuminates their own lack of rest. It can feel dangerous to seek this inner peace because this pursuit might be different from what your peers or family of origin want. You're still allowed to rest. Your commitment here is to yourself and meeting your needs so that you can move sustainably throughout your whole life, devoting your abundant energy to the things that matter most to you.

Journal prompts to dive deeper:

What beliefs do you carry about rest?

How has your need for rest shifted over the course of your life?

What are your feelings about your current rest needs?

What do you tell yourself is impossible about getting the rest you need?

What judgments do you carry about people who prioritize their need for rest?

> Curiously and lovingly ask yourself about your exhaustion.
> What is depleting you?
>
> Name the things that drain you and make a list. Give voice
> to this part of yourself without self-judgment or cruelty.

Running on Empty

What if just the thought of rest feels impossible? You might be working full-time as a single parent or currently taking care of a sick friend who requires around-the-clock attention. You might be working multiple jobs just to keep a roof over your head, driving from one to the other without a moment to yourself. You might be a stay-at-home parent with multiple children and never-ending piles of laundry. You might be a nurse or a mental health-care provider with more patients on your roster than you can attend to. You might be carrying more than any one human can reasonably be responsible for—with the added belief that rest is for the weak or the privileged. You might not yet know how to fit rest into your life, but that doesn't mean you require it any less. The practices in this chapter will encourage you to create pockets of rest whenever and wherever you can, including first thing in the morning, throughout the day, between meetings, before picking up your kids, and after your shift. These individual pockets of rest may not wholesale pull you out of your rest deficit, but with time they will add up and impact your energetic capacity.

In 2011, I came home from seeing clients and felt completely empty. I was in the middle of getting my graduate degree in social work while also completing my practicum as a therapist in a college counseling center. I walked through the door and plunked myself down on the couch. My partner had made me dinner, but I was too tired to eat it. They were excited to see me, but I had zero energy left to be excited about anything.

"Please," I said, "I can't hear or process another word today. Can we sit here and watch TV and then go to bed?" I fell asleep sitting up on the couch five minutes later.

My life didn't have to completely fall apart for me to become painfully aware it wasn't working. The truth was that at that moment I had nothing left to give. I had spent the first twenty-eight years of my life doing absolutely everything I believed was expected of me, preempting every request, completing every task as perfectly as possible, and I was suddenly unable to continue moving forward the way I had been. My actions had hinged on the belief that I was acceptable only when I was making myself profoundly useful to someone else. I was only lovable when I did it all. These beliefs kept me striving, terrified I would be rejected or abandoned if I slowed down or let anyone see how I really felt.

I didn't want to be the person who walked through the door without a drop of energy left for myself or my partner. I jealously compared myself to other people who seemed like they had it so much easier and were effortlessly able to do it all—care for themselves AND do everything else in their lives. *Why was I so broken? What was wrong with me? How could I possibly do more?* I was exhausted from a lifetime of overfunctioning and overachieving in a misbegotten attempt to earn something that could not be earned—my worth as a human being.

I understand, deeply, why we avoid our need for rest and how impossible it can be to prioritize it, as you crumble under the crushing pressure of needing to work to keep a roof over your head or to get your kids to school or just to keep moving to hold it all together. When you have borrowed against your own energy for years, it can feel as though your life is a stack of cards and even the slightest exhalation will cause everything you know and love to collapse. It can feel as though holding on tight and white-knuckling everything that has to be done is the safest option available. And yet, **everything** in your life becomes unsustainable if you do not tend to your need for rest.

If you're in this place, please hear me when I tell you that you not only need rest but also require it. You're rightfully exhausted. There is nothing wrong with you. You're a human living in late-stage capitalism, conditioned to believe that the best thing about you is what you achieve and produce for others. You may have even been taught that it is right and best to care for others and forgo your own rest. It will take time for you to unlearn all the stories bound up in your drive for unlimited productivity, but those conversations with yourself will require energy too. So first, you must rest. But what is rest exactly?

Defining Rest for Yourself

Rest is any activity that fills your cup or restores your energy. It's necessary because your energy determines your capacity for everything you want to make happen in your life. It's a baseline need, one that enables you to have the capacity for tending to other needs, and it requires energy to prioritize, which no doubt is one of the reasons you have resisted it for so long. You might ache for care because you're exhausted, but you don't have the energy to care for yourself. And that cycle keeps repeating as you fall deeper into a state of burnout. Paradoxically, front-loading rest will grant you more energy to use each day.

Let's start by talking about what rest is. Many people think of it narrowly as sleep. While sleep is important, it's not the only way we can infuse rest into our daily life. Meeting our need for rest is twofold. It includes both prioritizing restful moments and addressing the energy leaks that drain us. And as with safety, we all have unique rest needs too.

You might be coming to this work feeling burned-out on the idea of self-care, believing you've tried everything and nothing has made you feel any better after cruising through the many suggestions offered in the latest self-care article you read. But you're not a generic human. A generic list of ideas might give you a few things to try, but it's a paltry substitute for turning to yourself and asking what you really need. You might love taking a bubble bath, lighting a candle, and reading, or you might feel restored by doing something more physical like taking a walk outside. Moving your body involves an energy expenditure, but it is possible for moving your body to create more energy than the activity required. I personally find it restful to detail my car or to organize a small space. Although these activities have an energetic output, transforming a small space and doing something physical with my hands give me more energy than needed to complete the task.

The goal is to incorporate moments of reprieve into your daily life, instead of pushing rest to the bottom of your list after everything is done, which is to say, "never." If you're not attentive to your needs throughout the day, you're setting yourself up to be overwhelmed by them when you finish work. It's no surprise you feel like an overflowing bucket of neediness after you've gone through your day without thinking about your body or taking time for yourself.

Journal prompts to dive deeper:

Using this new definition of rest, what are your active rest activities? Make a list!

Using this new definition of rest, what are your passive rest activities? Make a list!

How might you incorporate more active rest into your daily life?

How might you incorporate more passive rest into your daily life?

What are you ready, able, and willing to say no to in order to say yes to rest?

Practice: Plugging Up Your Energy Leaks

The flip side of rest is stopping up the places in your life where you might be leaking energy, which requires a working understanding of your energetic capacity and what drains you. While society encourages us to see ourselves as all having equal amounts of energy (and that we can generate more if we hustle that little bit harder!), we all have a finite amount of energy each day. The amount of energy you have is specific to you and changes depending on your circumstances, season of life, hormonal fluctuations, and physical and mental health. What's more, different tasks require different amounts of energy for different people who all have individual experiences with those tasks. (You might find it easy to make a doctor's appointment, for example, while having a history of medical trauma might make that draining for me.)

Many of us navigate our lives with tiny energy leaks that go unseen but leave us drained by the end of the day. These might be boundaries (or a lack thereof), actions languishing on a to-do list that you don't really want to do, things that you might have said yes to but wanted to say no to, something you've been worrying about, or even the feeling you should be doing better than you are.

Plugging up these energy leaks is a tangible form of self-support. At first glance, it might not feel restful or restorative to call your student loan company, figure out that insurance policy, or set up a doctor's appointment, but these are the things that are subtly stressful and drain your energy, even when you aren't directly focused on them. Taking action to plug an energy leak may not seem restful when you're attending to it, but it will give you more energy in the long run.

START HERE

Pull out your journal and spend the next ten minutes making a list of everything that is draining your energy or exhausting you right now.

These might be tangible things like having to make a call or doing the books for your business, or they might be intangible things you aren't sure what to do with yet, such as having an uncomfortable conversation with your sibling about how you don't want to go on vacation with them this year. You don't have to understand the "how" of taking care of it right now. Just make the list.

When you're finished, look at your list and ask yourself: *What ONE thing on this list am I ready, able, and willing to address in order to plug that energy leak?*

Start with something simple and give yourself ample praise when you complete it. When you're ready, choose another thing off of the list. Don't forget to revel in how wonderful it feels to have that energy leak plugged up!

THIS MIGHT LOOK LIKE . . .

If you're at the self-responsibility stage, this might look like taking a moment to put your hand on your heart and express gratitude to yourself for everything you've been holding.

If you're at the self-care stage, this might look like reading through this list and understanding you need a lot more rest than you've been allowing yourself.

If you're at the self-trust stage, this might look like a moment of reckoning as you look at this list and realize *some* of what you've been pouring energy into or holding isn't yours to hold.

If you're at the self-love stage, this might look like gladly curling up for a little nap when you realize you are in need of one.

If you're at the advocacy stage, this might look like creating a weekly labor map with your partner, housemates, or coworkers. This map outlines absolutely EVERYTHING that must be done over the course of the week, including the emotional labor that is often overlooked. Emotional labor is the mental activity required to tend to the well-being of relationships and smooth management of household or project. After you figure out what all the moving parts are, have a conversation about how to divvy up the labor, depending on available time, energy, scheduling, and other commitments. What does each person *want* to contribute? How can you create an equal division of labor that dovetails with your individual strengths? These conversations might be uncomfortable at first, but they're powerful when put into routine practice. When Rae began this practice with her partner, it was eye-opening for both of them to see how much she was doing and holding over the course of the week! It was little wonder she was exhausted. Shining a light on the inner workings of what it *actually* took to run their household enabled them to more equally divide labor and appreciate each other for their efforts.

Cycle of Rest and Creation

Now let's zoom out a little from the micro view of capacity and energy leaks to look at the macro view of energetic balance. In many self-improvement circles there is discussion about working to find that elusive work-life balance—the magical place where everything seems effortless and lovely, while also joyfully productive. I don't believe in work-life balance, at least not in the way it's typically presented. I prefer instead to imagine a cycle of rest and creation, where you focus on how you're using your energy each day and how you're restoring the energy you have used.

First you rest, and then you create.

First you tend, and then you serve.

First you give to yourself, and then you give to others.

Rest
Restore
energy

Do + Create
use
energy

This cycle shows us that energy restoration isn't more important than energy use, nor energy use more important than energy restoration. Instead, what is essential is striking an imperfect balance between the two, so that you can continue to use your energy on the tasks and projects that matter to you in a way that is sustainable.

The cycle of rest and creation breaks the twenty-four-hour day into two halves. The first half is spent using your energy. It begins when you wake up and includes all of the things you do over the course of the day, where you expend energy until your energetic tank feels relatively empty. Then comes the opportunity to complete the other half of the cycle, restoring your energy. Restoring your energy includes restful activities that leave you with more energy than they require.

These two parts of the cycle work together, with you using your energy over the course of the day and then turning your attention to restoring your energy so that you have the capacity to begin again in the morning. It's useful to think about this cycle taking place in a twenty-four-hour period, even knowing it will often be impossible to strike a fifty-fifty balance here. This protects us from waiting until we are in an energy emergency to start taking care of ourselves or banking our care on the weekends, during a vacation, or waiting until conditions improve before taking care of ourselves. It is important to note here that your rest needs are not static, and it is understandable to require more rest at times. Your rest needs will change during different seasons of your life depending on what you have on your plate, your physical, mental, and emotional health. Because this is rarely spoken about in a positive light, you might muscle through your exhaustion or judge your increased need for rest. But there is no right or wrong amount of rest to need. We all have different rest needs, and there is very little use in fighting yours. Instead, learning what works best for you will enable you to rest and create in right timing for your body and life circumstances.

Journal prompts to dive deeper:

What beliefs do you carry about what it means to be productive?

What beliefs do you carry about what it means to work hard?

Where in your life do you routinely overextend yourself?

What is the benefit of overextending yourself?

What is the cost of overextending yourself?

What are you afraid might happen if you begin to prioritize rest?

Practice: Your Daily To-Do List Makeover

What would be different for you if you could check in with yourself, your body, and your energetic capacity before deciding what to work on and how to go about it? What would change if you gave yourself permission to be who and how you are instead of forcing your human feelings and needs to the edges of your life so that you can get more done?

When you opened this book, you already had a life constructed of previous commitments and circumstances. At this moment you might feel unable to make large changes in how you're approaching your life to make space for your needs—and that's totally okay. This exercise builds upon your daily check-in to facilitate a conversation with yourself about how to show up for whatever is on your plate. The concept is applicable whether you tend to create literal to-do lists or not because it is really about undermining perfectionism, managing our expectations for ourselves and getting into right relationship with the number of things we have set out to do each day.

The truth is, we either plan for our humanity or not doing so will wreck our plans, because we will never be able to permanently outrun our needs. Your to-do makeover list isn't inherently about doing less but instead giving yourself permission to be human and approaching your day responsive to how you feel ON THAT DAY—not on some generic, mythical, or rare day when you're firing on all cylinders and feeling incredible with the sun shining and everything going your way. Instead, as you are. On that day.

START HERE

Begin by checking in with yourself, taking the time to connect with yourself as you ask how you feel and what you need on this day. This enables you not only to think creatively about how and when you might be able to tend to your needs but also to better gauge how much you might reasonably expect yourself to accomplish this day.

Ask yourself: How do I feel today?

One day you might wake up feeling fantastic and well rested, capable of tackling the harder things on your to-do list or the energy leaks you've been avoiding. Another day you might wake up feeling dehydrated and exhausted, knowing these conditions will reduce your capacity for doing things, so you give yourself permission to move more slowly or to take extra breaks for drinking water. Both of these are examples of choosing to be responsive to your body and needs when making your plans for the day.

Ask yourself: Based on how I feel, what do I need today?

After checking in with your needs, choose what you're going to focus on today, limiting yourself to three activities. Yes, you might want to get more than three things done, but the possibility of overwhelming yourself into inaction increases as you raise your expectations for yourself. Be kind to yourself by keeping your focus as simple and clear as possible. Make sure the things you choose are tasks a real live human can accomplish in a day.

Ask yourself: Based on how I feel and what I need, what do I have the intention and capacity to accomplish today? Write those three things down.

Next, create a boundary for yourself by choosing an end point— either the number of things you're going to accomplish, a time you're going to stop, or some other predetermined end point—for the active work part of your day. This active work might include your job, work you do from home, volunteer work, and work you do in and around your home. I am defining *work* as anything that requires more energy to accomplish than you receive (*aka* the opposite of a restful activity).

Ask yourself: When is my end point? How will I restore my energy once I'm done working?

Restful activities give you more energy than they require to complete

"WORK activities" use more energy than they require to complete

There will never be a time when you run out of things you feel responsible for. Creating a container around your work and your commitments for the day enables you to free yourself up for self-tending or doing something joyful to restore your energy when work is over. And really follow through—don't blow past your end points, or fall into the trap of "just one more thing." You deserve better.

One thing to be especially aware of is the tendency to use up all our reserves before resting and replenishing. So many of us have the feeling that we have to wring every drop of energy out of ourselves in service of being productive, good, or effective, when that's just not true. You deserve to have a surplus of energy, and you deserve to use that surplus for things that delight and support you. Give yourself more than the scraps.

Like everything in this book, this is a process of learning. Trying. Falling and getting back up again. Doing it "wrong" and then figuring out what you really want. As you do the work of this book, you'll gain a better understanding of *why* you want to do certain things with your energy. Ultimately, this book is about helping you answer the question "How do I want to live?" And that takes time, energy, and practice.

The very last step is to give some thought to how you will restore your energy when you're done working for the day. You might not yet know, but it's worthwhile to begin your day thinking about how you might restore your energy after working. What will you feed yourself for dinner? How will you tend to your body this afternoon or evening? Will you check in with yourself again at your end point to ask yourself what might feel good? There are wonderful options for restoring your energy, but ultimately the decision lands in your lap as you respond to your needs at the end of the day.

THIS MIGHT LOOK LIKE . . .

If you're at the self-responsibility stage, this might look like realizing how much you've been expecting of yourself each day. Yikes! No wonder you haven't been able to get it all done.

If you're at the self-care stage, this might look like matching your care to the level of things on your plate. Remember, the more energy you spend, the more energy you need to replenish.

If you're at the self-trust stage, this might look like feeling safe doing less—even when it's uncomfortable—because you trust yourself to pick it back up tomorrow when you're well rested again.

If you're at the self-love stage, this might look like realizing your plate is STILL full, even though you've cleared it of a lot of the things you previously said yes to but didn't really want to do. Our excited, full-body yeses pile up too! So we still need to set boundaries with ourselves, even when we are utterly enthusiastic about the projects in front of us.

If you're at the advocacy stage, this might look like getting curious about what support you need to accomplish your priorities. No one said you have to get there alone! What assistance would make the process that much more possible or pleasurable?

Rest Rebels and Tending to Conflicting Needs

If you find yourself really struggling with rest, I invite you to get curious about what is standing between you and the rest you need. What are the obstacles you never quite seem to get around? There isn't something personally wrong with you because you can't get to bed earlier. You're a complex human with many needs to respond to at any given moment. Oftentimes we experience the need for rest alongside a competing need, such as finishing just one more thing to get ready for tomorrow, spending time with our partner, or finally getting a moment to ourselves to unwind.

Each morning Andrea promised herself that night would be the night she finally got to bed early. She was exhausted. She had been exhausted for as long as she could remember. But when it came time to get into bed at night, she found herself with a million reasons why she should do anything but that. She would fold laundry, rearrange her refrigerator, press play on episode after episode of her favorite TV show, and if she did climb into bed on time, she would find herself scrolling through social media for hours.

"It isn't fair," she told me. After getting home from work, eating dinner with her partner, and cleaning up the kitchen, those late-night hours were the only moments she had either to get things done or to do something nice for herself. She didn't want to waste those precious moments on sleep. When Andrea and I started working together, two things were clear: she was exhausted, and something was keeping her from honoring her desire to get more rest at night. As we pulled back the layers, it became clear that Andrea wasn't honoring her needs over the course of the day—in fact, she was operating in quite the opposite way. She would get up, get to work, work late into the evening, come home and work at home, and then she didn't want to get into bed. She was experiencing conflicting needs for rest and for play, pleasure, autonomy, and more. She was allowing herself to be a human only after everything else was done, and unfortunately that was already bedtime. As she started carving out more moments for rest and play throughout the day—by drinking her coffee outside on her deck, singing along to her favorite music on the way to work, setting boundaries at work to leave on time, connecting with her husband while they ate dinner, and creating a luxurious pre-bedtime routine—she stopped seeing going to bed at a reasonable hour as a punishment.

Nighttime might be the only time you have to yourself, so you want to use it for your own devices. In a world where productivity is king and we pray at the altar of busyness, "work" hours are deemed nonnegotiable, forcing our many needs to be met around the periphery of work. You might think, *I finally have some time for myself. I don't just want to get into bed to sleep.* During these peripheral hours, rest competes with joy, community, celebration, and nourishment, to name just a few. These competing needs are incredibly important to acknowledge, and the more you turn your attention to your expectations for your own productivity and the boundaries needed between work and rejuvenation, the more space you will have to attend to those needs, and not in the thirty minutes before bed.

The time between work and rest can be a tender time. If you have been avoiding your needs during the day, it's a time when you encounter your neediness and might feel too overwhelmed and exhausted to make choices that support you. But what if you were to choose rest over checking Facebook one more time? How might it feel to take a long shower and imagine that everything that no longer serves you is being washed down the drain, instead of slowly melting into the couch? What would be different for you if you spent five minutes writing in your journal, so that you don't have to hold all your thoughts together in your head all the time? What if you shut off your phone for an hour and read a book? How might you arrive at work if you've spent your commute gleefully scream-singing along with your favorite song? These small acts of reprieve have enormous impacts on how you feel.

Press Pause and Rest

While it can be challenging to unlearn the belief that you need to tick every box or wipe every surface before you surrender to sleep, meeting your need for rest is well worth the discomfort of grappling with these beliefs.

A beautiful way to reframe the urgency around doing it all and earning your rest is to think about pressing pause on whatever it is you are working on or using as the reason you cannot rest when you are truly exhausted. Will you be able to do this all of the time? No. Of course not. You will encounter busy seasons and deadlines when you might be putting out more energy than you are recouping each day. But let those moments be the exception. Whenever possible, remind yourself that regenerating your energetic capacity is essential. You are a human, and humans require rest. Press pause. Whatever you're tussling with will be there in the morning.

Commitments to My Need for Rest

— I'm allowed to rest. Even if. Even when. No matter what. Rest is a requirement, and I'm allowed to have it.

— Rest doesn't always mean inaction. Instead, it's those activities that fill my cup. I move through cycles of rest and creation, each feeding the other.

— It's always a good idea to get a sense of my energetic leaks to better meet my rest needs. I might be pouring water into a leaky cup without realizing it.

— As counterintuitive as it may sound, if I've created a life for myself where I'm so burned-out and overscheduled that the last thing I have time for is rest, then I need to rest. In this instance (and many others) it's the most productive thing I can do.

— What about conflicting needs? If I find myself rebelling against rest or avoiding it, that's completely normal. As with everything, I will start small. Do what I can. And keep doing it. Rest, then create. Tend, then do. Care, then act.

CHAPTER 4

Sustenance

BLESSING

Your body is not an ornament or a vehicle. It is a vessel. Your life is not a foregone conclusion. It lives and breathes beneath your touch.

You may carry a legacy of ignored needs. You may carry the burden of feeling burdensome—too much, not enough, and always searching for The Thing. You may be exhausted from trying to fix something that was never actually broken. You may wonder if the sustenance you ache for is even possible for you.

It is.

Your needs are not a burden. Your needs are sacred.

Upon waking, climb into your body and ask yourself what is needed most. Learn how to meet your needs by practicing. Devote yourself to imperfectly meeting the needs that arise in whatever way you're able. Conduct your life from the center of it instead of pressing yourself against the edges in an effort not to be seen. This reconfiguration is both an immense shift and a very simple realignment in how you spend your daily energy.

Choose yourself, even when choosing yourself feels impossible, rebellious, and selfish. Reimagine the purpose of your life—living instead of producing, pleasing yourself instead of seeking external validation.

You don't have to do it all at once. You don't have to make a huge transition or declaration. Tending to yourself—centering yourself in your own life—is a practice of paying attention and taking the time to respond to your needs as they arise. It isn't something reserved for people who are more special, intelligent, well-off, or successful than you. It isn't something you "get" for having "made it." Being well nourished, lit up, and supported is your birthright.

There is nothing for you to earn here.

> I want to find people like me. Brave people. People
> who are doing the work to revere their bodies
> in a world that shuns and discards bodies that
> look like mine. People who want to talk about the
> politics of how we reclaim our identities from
> the conveyor belt perfectionism puts us on.

WHEN I STARTED MY FIRST BLOG in 2008, I was hungry for a conversation that, until that point, I had only had with myself. Long before body positivity washed ashore on my sleepy peninsula, I was hard at work unlearning the conditioning that disconnected me from my body. I thought if I started to write about it and followed other people's online writing, maybe I would find some people who wanted to talk about this with me. I soon started long-distance conversations with brilliant humans like Amber Karnes, founder of Body Positive Yoga; Anna Guest-Jelley, founder of Curvy Yoga; Rosie Molinary, author of *Beautiful You: A Daily Guide to Radical Self-Acceptance* and *Hijas Americanas: Beauty, Body Image, and Growing Up Latina;* among others. Their voices bolstered something that was being born in me, and immediately I felt less alone.

More than companionship, I was hungry to be met with the specific beliefs I was learning to hold true for myself—namely, that my worth isn't contingent upon the size of my body, and then later, that my worth isn't married to my productivity or perfection. I devoured blog posts, books, and podcasts that spoke to this burgeoning self-belief, feeling my connection with my true and essential self being strengthened with each bite.

When I started my podcast, *Needy,* it was because my clients kept telling me that before working with me they had never heard anyone discuss needs in a positive or even neutral light. As I gathered communities together to teach them about healing our relationships with our bodies, needs, and hungers, I realized that the most powerful part of these learning environments was the shared experience of realizing that having needs isn't a shameful secret. It doesn't make us weak, too sensitive, or unlovable. When we bear witness to one another's neediness, we are able to soften into our shared experience of being the inconvenient, glorious, messy humans we ALL are.

This is one way we feed ourselves: by immersing ourselves in communities of shared values. But of course there are more, and that's what this chapter is about.

What Is Sustenance?

Connecting to your need for sustenance invites you to build upon our previous work with safety and rest as you begin working with the foundation of identifying and prioritizing actions that satisfy you versus attempting to fill yourself with paltry substitutes that leave you feeling frustrated, lonely, and unappreciated.

Your need for sustenance relates to the grounding energy center at the base of your tailbone. The root of your body is connected to the feelings of safety and security you experience when you trust that your needs are important and will be met. The need for sustenance isn't necessarily about the individual needs themselves but about satisfying the deep craving for *consistency* in having your needs met. You crave the acts of care in and of themselves, but you also crave mattering enough to be cared for every single day without having to earn it. Sustenance is about meeting the need for whatever nourishes you—your hungers, your desires, your particular needs and preferred ways of doing things. Meeting the need for sustenance is about feeding yourself or being fed by whatever it is you are hungry for.

Alone time. A five-minute daily creative practice.
Soft clothing. Fresh air and a beautiful view.
A weekend away with your best friends—having a
close circle of friends to begin with! Inspiration.
A deeper intimacy with yourself or your partner(s).

Tending to your voracious appetite for mattering
and the robust certainty from weaving examples
of that mattering into your daily life.

Katrina began working with me to get to the bottom of her jealousy of a friend. She wanted to take responsibility for her feelings and remain friends with this person, but when she was really honest with herself, after they spent time together she would leave seething. In our sessions, Katrina would rant about how this friend took up so much space, treated herself to luxurious experiences, asked for exactly what she wanted, and got it! Katrina and I spoke at length about what her friend had that she desperately wanted for herself. While she wanted many of the external things that her friend had, what Katrina *really* wanted was to feel as though she had permission to prioritize the things that lit her up too. She felt compelled by her friend's freedom and confidence to pursue whatever delighted her. She was hungry for that kind of permission to pursue what was joyful and restorative for her.

When I asked Katrina what she would prioritize if she felt she had permission, she paused before admitting she had never given it much thought because she assumed it was impossible, so why bother. But as she thought about her friend and a recent trip she had taken for the weekend, Katrina offered that up as an example of something that appealed to her. She started to describe a beautiful boutique hotel with a view of the ocean and interesting art hanging in each room. She had wanted to go away there for a weekend for years but had never carved out the time. "Start with that," I urged her, "and each step along the way, ask yourself what you really want"—*for breakfast, to listen to on the car ride there, for dinner, to do at night, to wear to bed, to do for fun.* The options were endless.

What are you longing for?

What nourishes you?

These questions are at the core of honoring your need for sustenance, but they might be tender to navigate. Your longing might be a visceral, physical hunger or it might be a spiritual, emotional, or erotic hunger. You might not yet know what deeply nourishes you. Are you hungry for food, color, inspiration, sensuality, a greater sense of safety, or purpose? This hunger relates to both the actual desire itself and also the creativity you harness in how you approach it. Your hunger might be less about the thing itself and more about the process of journeying from here to there. Tending to your need for sustenance is about showing up for these desires **and** taking the time to make each experience as enjoyable as possible, because each and every time you offer this generosity to yourself, you reinforce the fledgling belief that you're worth caring for, loving, and prioritizing.

Meeting your need for sustenance is about feeding yourself what you're hungry for instead of what you think you should want or deserve. Feeding your body, mind, and spirit in this way not only sustains your energy but is also generative.

In the last chapter, we discussed energy use and awareness of the energy tax that accompanies particularly challenging tasks. In a similar concept, nourishing yourself creates a surplus of energy. Cultivating a life that is specifically supportive and life-affirming for YOU in particular generates more energy than any of the individual acts of care require. This is about feeding yourself, but it is about so much more. It is about the experience of feeling seen, heard, and supported, which accompanies caring for yourself in a particular, bespoke way. This is where we begin to put the data we acquire when we give ourselves permission to rest to good use, using it to create care opportunities that are as unique as our particular flavor of needs.

Journal prompts to dive deeper:

What nourishes you?

What is your body hungry for?

What is your mind ready for?

> What is your heart longing for?
>
> What is your spirit aching for?

The End of All-or-Nothing, Emergency Self-Care

What message are you giving to yourself when you wait until you're in crisis before you begin caring for yourself? I used to be deeply entrenched in this pattern. I'd care for myself just enough so that I could be productive again and then get back to work until my next care emergency. I'd crash from striving and producing without a thought to my needs and then stop just long enough to treat myself just kindly enough to nurse myself back to health so that I could resume my breakneck speed.

Those days were exhilarating because even in my burnout I felt so purposeful, high on how good I was at pushing my needs aside to tackle whatever needed tackling. Exceptionally good in a crisis, I felt born for running myself into the ground and then picking up the pieces just enough to get back to work. Even as this pattern started to break down for me, I could feel my ego attachment to it. I was good at getting things done. I was good at helping others. I was good at putting everyone else's needs ahead of my own. I was good. I was good. I was good.

The tricky thing about this pattern is that needs will get met one way or another. They don't just vanish or disappear when you ignore them. They become rowdier and rowdier, nipping at your heels as you try to outrun them. Your body is infinitely wise and makes more noise as your ache for care compounds itself. When you ignore your needs long enough, you will be forced to prioritize yourself by circumstance, illness, or burnout, bringing you abruptly to the crisis point of having to slow down.

But even in the face of that, attending to the need for sustenance can sometimes still feel impossible if you are exhausted from a lifetime of holding it all together. While the need for sustenance might seem to come before rest, I ordered these chapters deliberately, because having the energy to start asking big questions about what you need requires energy too. You're crumbling beneath the weight of your conditioned expectations for yourself and others, and you judge yourself for not being about to do it all without a thought for the energetic capacity necessary to prioritize joy, pleasure, or satiety. You might think, *Well if it's right, it should feel good or it should be easy.* But tending to your needs can be almost boring, and having the capacity to investigate the larger picture of what you are hungry for requires energy. It requires stamina and self-awareness to develop a healthy relationship with yourself after being in a dysfunctional relationship—one that's chaotic, intense, familiar, thrilling, and compelling even when you know there is no way it will all work out in the long run. After a dramatic relationship like that, a relationship in which you are respectful of each other, loyal, trustworthy, and committed to each other can feel boring—but that kind of steadfast love heals and rebuilds a steady foundation of trust. The same is true for your relationship with yourself.

> Self-love so often isn't a flash-in-the-pan,
> Instagram-worthy, *wait-until-the-moment-*
> *is-perfect-and-the-stars-align* kind of love.

It's about showing up for yourself each and every day and doing what needs to be done. Maybe that's resting. Maybe that's calling your lawyer. Maybe that's dealing with the window that is leaking and the moldy floorboards. Taking care of yourself is showing up for your relationship with yourself each day, asking what needs to be done and doing that to the best of your abilities.

It can be mundane, but as you begin making these shifts for your own sustenance, you might find yourself softening into a rhythm and routine of caring for yourself this way. There is a deliciousness in knowing you will be there when you need yourself. There is a sense of safety in the self-trust you build each time you choose not to abandon yourself.

This work can be messy but also joyful, silly, sexy, creative, and playful. You might find yourself enjoying the celebration of infusing pleasure and sovereignty where there was none before.

And with time, you might realize that the purpose of your life is not to be good, productive, or approved by others. The purpose of your life is for YOU to live it. For you to take up space in your own thoughts and actions. For you to tend to your needs, devoting yourself to your own wholeness each and every day. For you to contribute to the world in the way that only you can. For you to love and be loved. For you to play. For your utter enjoyment and wholehearted pleasure. The purpose of your life is not to be nice and polite. It is for living—messily, humanly, in whatever way you feel is good and right for you.

Practice: Honoring and Identifying Burnout Warning Signs

An important aspect of knowing when and how to care for yourself is the practice of seeing the warning signs that you're in need of support from a greater and greater distance. Your exhaustion, emotional fragility, reactivity, overwhelm, explosive anger, and boiling resentment are not character flaws. They are warning signs. They are symptoms of your lack of care, pointing you toward your inherent neediness. An essential practice for finding your way out of the pattern of emergency self-care is bringing your attention to your need for care when your body is whispering for your attention instead of waiting until it is yelling and demanding you take notice.

When I came to this work, I imagined that "being healed" would look like no longer needing to pay attention to myself. I fantasized that I would get so good at taking care of myself I would be able to put my relationship with myself on autopilot and return to working on important things again. That hasn't been the case. Instead, I have learned that healing doesn't mean we get to some magical destination point; instead, our self-care becomes more nuanced. With time, we're able to identify our need for care sooner, and we heed our own call to turn toward ourselves before it becomes an emergency. This model of healing is relational. I am in a relationship with myself, which means I am always in the process of monitoring how I'm doing. I slow down when my body asks me to slow down, rest when my body needs rest, and care for myself before I crumble at my own feet. If life is hectic and I cannot immediately tend to my needs, I take a moment to validate the presence of my needs and plan to tend to them in whatever way is doable as soon as I can. As you work with this concept, you will become more adept at seeing the warning signs from a distance, responding more quickly, and ultimately reducing instances of burnout, resentment, and exhaustion.

START HERE

Part One

Pull out your notebook and work through the following journal prompts, spending a few minutes on each one. If you aren't sure about your answer to one of the questions, keep moving. Start with what you do know and lean into whatever data reveals itself.

Feelings:

> What feelings show up when I am exhausted or burned out?
>
> What feelings show up more often when I need tending?
>
> What feelings indicate my boundaries have been trespassed?

Behaviors:

> What behaviors or patterns indicate I need my own care?
>
> What do I notice myself doing to try to meet my needs that might miss the mark or not actually meet the need it is intended to meet?

What behaviors show up when my boundaries have been trespassed?

Physical Sensations:

What physical warning signs let me know I need care?

What does burnout or exhaustion feel like in my body?

How does my body feel when my boundaries have been trespassed?

What physiological sensations indicate the need to slow down or ask for support?

Part Two

Now it is time to organize the data. Take your lists and begin to organize your feelings, behaviors, and physical sensations along a spectrum of low need to high need. A low need might be a small indicator that you're in need of care—a sensitivity to noise, feeling more tired or weepy than usual, taking things more personally than you might otherwise. A high need would be a larger indicator that you're in need of care—screaming at the other cars during rush hour, fighting with your partner over everything, wanting to run away from your life, or feeling personally attacked when someone asks you to do something.

Creating your own system for categorizing these feelings, behaviors, and physical sensations will help you gain awareness of how they alert you to your need for tending, and it is a powerful tool for caring for yourself with greater confidence and regularity. Hang this list where you will see it often. Familiarize yourself with the warning signs and incorporate them into your daily or weekly check-ins with yourself. The more often you bring your awareness here, the more easily you will tend to yourself proactively and ward off the more overwhelming experiences of burnout.

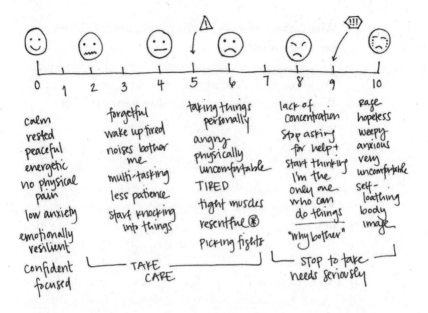

THIS MIGHT LOOK LIKE . . .

If you're at the self-responsibility stage, this might look like beginning to realize you've been reading your warning signs as personal failures or weaknesses and using them as fodder to work even harder. Cue more burnout and more warning signs!

If you're at the self-care stage, this might look like gaining a greater awareness of where on the scale you really need to turn your attention to your own care. Where do things tend to go from not awesome to really bad? Put a star or exclamation point at this tipping point and make sure you pay attention to it in the future.

If you're at the self-trust stage, this might look like understanding how much easier it is to communicate and partner with yourself when your warning signs are lower.

If you're at the self-love stage, this might look like having compassion for the times in your life when you allowed yourself to become all too comfortable at level 10 burnout and expressing gratitude to yourself for the powerful understanding that this is not the place where you can contribute, relate, or show up the way you want to.

If you're at the advocacy stage, this might look like saying no when you are nearing the burned-out end of the spectrum. It might also look like honoring your needs by offering accurate timelines for projects and plans on your plate and saying, "I would be happy to, but it will take me until [insert timing] to get it back to you." This was the case for Connor, who struggled to say no when put on the spot, especially at work. Instead of waiting until this felt more comfortable, Connor developed a short script that enabled them to have a few moments to determine whether they had the capacity to fulfill a request and the timeline they could promise. Whenever put on the spot, Connor would say, "Let me check my [calendar/to-do list/whatever was relevant] and let you know later today."

Sustenance and Gratitude

What does gratitude have to do with sustenance? Everything. If your gratitude doesn't include gratitude for yourself and everything you accomplish, withstand, and digest on a daily basis, it is incomplete. Gratitude and enoughness are partners: one lifts you up, and the other determines the container. When we cultivate self-gratitude, we practice acknowledging our efforts as worthy and good, even when they are imperfect or incomplete. The more we can appreciate our efforts, the easier it is to replenish the energy a task requires. If you're arriving here with an energetic deficit, your first task isn't to belittle yourself and further burden yourself with a continuation of the cultural story that you just can't hack it. Your first task is to amplify your gratitude for yourself.

Speak these words aloud:

> Wow! Look how much I have done.
>
> Wow! I have been working really hard for a really long time. I am amazing. I am astonished by how much I have accomplished with so few personal resources.
>
> I have moved mountains, created humans in my body, written five bajillion grants [insert what you've done here, of course].
>
> I am a phenomenal creator.

Be generous with your affirmations and acknowledgement.

This sustenance might feel profoundly uncomfortable at first. You may need to remind yourself again and again that you're allowed to receive it regardless of what you've done to "deserve it." Surround yourself with sticky notes or reminders on your phone—whatever works to remind you to soften and receive. Tell yourself: *I have done enough. I am enough. I was always more than enough. I am allowed to take care of myself. There is nothing to strive for here.* Many of us have not been taught to appreciate ourselves or to relish our endeavors. Instead, we are sold the lie that approval is meaningless and untrustworthy unless it comes from a source outside ourselves—a lie that sets us up for a lifetime of striving for other people's approval.

We care for what we deem worthy of care, and it is little wonder that so many of us struggle to believe we have earned the right to our own care. The self-care industry as a whole doesn't help with this because it lauds care that is meant to improve us in some way, continually moving the goalpost so that standards are impossible to reach. Again, we are told that we are worthy of our own care but ONLY if said care activity improves us in some way—making us more patient, productive, sexy, loving, kind, or interesting. Such care activities do not set us free to enjoy the pleasure and life-generating experience of tending to ourselves in whatever way feels best. Listicles outlining "10 Self-Care Actions You Can Do Right Now" subtly tell us:

You're a thing to be fixed. You may engage in
care that makes you better, smarter, or more
lovely, but then you better get back to work.

We are taught that filling ourselves with gratitude will lead to happier
and healthier lives. We are told to list the things we are grateful for in
notebooks by our beds or on little pieces of paper to exorcise the darkness from our lives and fill each corner with light. We are not taught to
experience or verbalize gratitude for *ourselves*.

Journal prompts to dive deeper:

What feelings or thoughts come up when you think
about expressing gratitude to yourself for everything
you are doing well?

What stories or beliefs come up when you imagine
celebrating yourself or turning your attention to what
you appreciate about yourself?

Are you treating yourself as sacred?

What does sacred treatment look like?

What are you afraid might happen if you grant yourself
grace and self-compassion in this way?

Doing What Is Doable: The Five Minutes
in the Bathroom That Saved My Life

I was working with a client who said, "When you talk about your self-
care, it sounds like a full-time job! I can't understand how you find
the time. I barely have five minutes to myself." I laughed because it's
true, taking care of myself and making sure my needs for sustenance
are met ARE a full-time job. But it didn't start out that way. Ten years

ago, I remember feeling the same way my client felt. I knew I needed my own care, but I had no idea where to start. I felt so broken, overwhelmed, and disconnected from myself that I was unaware it was even possible to show up differently in my life. Because I was disconnected from my body, I was also disconnected from my hungers. I did not know how to provide myself with the sustenance I needed. I didn't even know what I needed.

This is just how it is, I told myself. *This is just what being an adult is like. I should be grateful. Overall my life is pretty good. Someone loves me. I'm doing an okay job at work. Yeah sure, I'm tired, but who isn't? I should be working harder to take care of my body. I'm doing the best I can, even though it never ever feels like enough.* I told myself it was okay, but I knew it wasn't. I knew from somewhere deep inside myself that my life wasn't supposed to be about lining up a bunch of perfect-looking successes— degree, private practice, marriage, children—but my exhaustion was a thick fog blanketing everything in my life, so that when I heard my inner voice, it was garbled, distant, and untrustworthy.

When I came to terms with the fact that the way I had structured my life wasn't working, I made the choice to find ONE small step to start taking care of myself. I decided that twice a day, in the morning and evening, I would walk into the bathroom, close the door, and spend five minutes washing my face and brushing my teeth. I wouldn't take my phone into the bathroom with me. I wouldn't check my emails while brushing my teeth. I wouldn't talk to my partner through the open door while washing my face about our schedule for the day. I would close the door and wash my face and brush my teeth in solitude.

I can't tell you how revolutionary those five minutes were. It felt like I was stealing important time from my own productivity. Wasn't the point to maximize every moment of the day so that I could get the most done possible, in the constant endeavor to work my way to the bottom of my forever list so that I could FINALLY find some time off to take care of myself? It turned out, no. That was not the point. That was my conditioning, and my conditioning was keeping me from feeling I deserved five minutes of my own time and attention—five minutes to check in with my needs and see what I was actually hungry for.

This inner work begins with choosing yourself each day and reminding yourself that you are worthy of the effort that honoring your needs requires. Choose to see your needs as worthy of your attention—so worthy that they deserve failing or floundering or the messiness of beginning again (and again and again).

You don't need someone else to tell you *how* to take care of yourself. Just as your body will tell you what food it wants, your body, heart and intuition will tell you what you need for sustenance, but you have to be open to receiving the information even when it differs from your beautifully laid plans. The more you listen to the wisdom dwelling in your skin, the more at home you will feel, and the louder that voice will become.

Some people like to check in with themselves first thing in the morning while still lying in bed. Others prefer a meeting with themselves over a cup of coffee. I find a particular delight in taking a few minutes to slow down and connect with myself as I transition from work to home life in the evening. What time of day could you use more support? Start there. Use that moment to ask yourself the question, *What do I need right now?* Ask with an open heart and give yourself permission to change your mind. Prioritize whatever shows up, whatever need is asking to be met. Keep it simple. Do not overwhelm yourself into a place of inaction.

I started with those five minutes of flossing and brushing. I used those minutes to check in with myself, look myself in the eye in the mirror, and bear witness to my needs and hungers. There were many moments when I wanted to look away or felt overwhelmed by my neediness, but I made the choice to hear myself out, even when I knew meeting a particular need would be impossible that day. This practice reinforced my belief that I was allowed to have needs and that my needs weren't too much. I could bear the sight of myself—imperfect, human, and needy.

Journal prompts to dive deeper:

What need(s) have you been avoiding or pushing to the side for a more convenient time?

What needs feel impossible to meet?

How do you benefit from avoiding those needs?

What are the costs of continuing to avoid or ignore your needs?

What is one small, doable step you can take to meet an inconvenient need today?

Your Realm of Responsibility

You may be coming up against some powerful beliefs about not having the time or space to support your needs for sustenance, even as you ache for that care. You might be wondering about your conflicting needs or how to balance what you hunger for with the energy you typically spend caring for other humans' needs—your children, your partner, your boss, your best friend, whichever humans you check in with regularly and prioritize above your own needs. When do those get met? Are those even your responsibility? Who are you if you aren't the person responsible for doing ALL THE THINGS ALL THE TIME? Who will you become if you slow down to ask for and get the sustenance you need?

The truth is, not having time or space in your life to sustain and nourish yourself is a boundary issue, both in your relationships with others **and** in your relationship with yourself. A boundary is the delineation between what is yours and what is not. It is a communication about what you are available for and what you require in order to feel safe, secure, and supported in a relationship. Defining your realm of responsibility is a practice in articulating for yourself what you are ready, able, and willing to claim responsibility for, instead of assuming you are responsible for everything. This practice will help you examine how you're spending your energy each day and return some of the responsibilities you shoulder back to their original and rightful owners.

Let's walk our way back to the plots of land that represent our inner landscapes. That land is your realm of responsibility, and it is up to you to steward it in such a way that you can get the sustenance you need. This realm includes your thoughts, feelings, actions, reactions, the consequences of your actions, and your daily choices. I like to think of it as a plot of land surrounded by a fence, a boundary, that includes a gate. You're the sovereign leader and determine what is permitted entry and exit. The border around your inner landscape is comprised of your boundaries denoting what is yours to tend to and what is not. The people who you share your life with might have adjacent properties. Your children might have their own small plots of land right outside of your fence, which grow in size as they grow. But you have to walk through your land to tend to them. You're first required to nourish and tend to what is yours before you make yourself available to anyone and anything outside yourself. This requires that you maintain a boundary.

This boundary is a flexible one, a semipermeable membrane that allows for the connection and shared experiences that enable you to thrive, and when intact, will also protect you from the unwanted opinions, actions, and reactions of others. Learning to tend to yourself and give yourself the sustenance you need means working to embody this boundary.

Here are some common ways you might dodge your responsibility for the boundaries that allow you to meet your need for sustenance.

I need XYZ, but they won't give it to me.

No one else is responsible for meeting your needs or holding your boundaries. You and you alone are responsible for your needs. There might be times when your need includes someone else in your life. You might, for example, desire closeness or physical intimacy with your partner. You might need to complete something that you need help completing. Your safety might be closely aligned with someone else's choices or behavior if you share a life or home with that person. Your job is to identify, honor, and advocate for your needs within your relationships. That other person may or may not be available to meet your needs, which has very little to do with you or your neediness and everything to do with their personal capacity at the moment. You're responsible for those needs whether or not that other person is available to join you in meeting them—and you can choose to shut down in the face of a no or to get creative about how you're going to meet that need.

As you begin to unearth your needs, you will reach a point where you are ready to share them with the people in your life. Asking is your realm of responsibility. For example, you might tell your partner you would like to prioritize more intimacy and sexual connection in your relationship. They get to respond whether or not they have the capacity to meet that need with you. Your needs are valid, and you are allowed to advocate for them. Determining whether or not your partner has the capacity to meet you in that need, however, is squarely within *their* realm of responsibility. It may not be a priority for them for a multitude of reasons, but none of those reasons mean you should have protected them from your asking. After asking, your responsibility is considering their response. If their response is that they don't have capacity to meet your needs in that moment, then it is your responsibility to consider how else you might get that need met. Perhaps you will compromise on a future time to meet that need. Each of us has our own level of tolerance for unmet needs, and if the other person is repeatedly unavailable for something you can't meet on your own or wait for, you might make a choice about how to continue that relationship. What is important to remember here is that it is your responsibility to advocate for what you need and someone else not having the capacity to meet it is not a referendum on the need itself but a mismatch in capacity, interest, or desire.

Sustaining myself is not possible because I'm so busy meeting everyone else's needs.

This lie is alluring because so many of us have been raised to believe it is our job to put everyone else's needs above our own, that doing so is what makes us good, valuable, and worthy. BIPOC, women, and people of all genders who were socialized as girls during childhood are told this story again and again by the world around them, their families of origin, the media, and the thick societal messaging we breathe from birth.

Navigating the stories and beliefs we hold about our worthiness is our responsibility. As we begin attending to the many ways our lives are unsustainable, it is essential we realize that doing for others at the expense of caring for ourselves is not our job. Reclaiming our energy to commit to our own care requires we examine our underlying motivations for putting others ahead of ourselves.

What's more, trying to micromanage someone else's process is a boundary violation, especially when you haven't been invited to do so. Jumping in or taking over someone else's process distracts you from the available time and energy to take care of yourself. Part of this work is disentangling from our enmeshment with other people and getting really clear about what our job is.

I can't feed myself what I need until I earn it.

Living, breathing, and working in a capitalist society conditions us to believe our value is directly associated with how much we produce and our proximity to the identity of an able-bodied, heterosexual, White, cisgendered male (the ideal for what constitutes a valuable human within our society). The further away our identities place us from that ideal, the more we are taught to work to make up for the perceived lack. This narrative is imprinted upon us every day of our lives in both subtle and explicit ways, but it is one we personally reinforce as we continue to carry and perpetuate these beliefs in our daily choices.

As individuals we may not be able to overturn centuries of power structures that impact our self-image and sense of possibility, but we can make strides to care for ourselves, even when it goes against our ingrained conditioning. We are tender stewards to the meaning we make of those realities and the ways we choose to learn to process and heal from these experiences. Each and every time you honor your need for rest and restoration, you teach yourself that your value is not in what you produce for others.

 ## Practice: Defining Your Realm of Responsibility

This practice will give you an opportunity to experiment with determining what is your responsibility and surrendering the things outside your control and area of impact, so you can build the good, strong fences that allow you to continually meet your need for sustenance.

Remember, you are responsible for your thoughts, feelings, actions, reactions, and the consequences of your actions. The other adults in your life are responsible for their thoughts, feelings, actions, reactions, and the consequences of their actions. If you have children, they are in a bit of a gray zone. Taking care of them is certainly your responsibility, but they are also born with free will and choice. Which means, it is your job to care for them, especially when they are very young, but not at the expense of caring for yourself because your care for them is only sustainable if you are well-tended.

Take a big piece of paper and draw a circle in the middle of it. Inside of that circle write "my responsibility," and in the area outside the circle write "not my responsibility."

Spend some time thinking about everything on your plate right now: everything you're worried about, consumed by, or struggling to hold. As you move through the different situations, relationships, and circumstances in your mind, ask yourself, *Is this my responsibility?* If yes, write it inside your circle; if not, write it outside your circle.

Certain issues that contain both personal and collective responsibilities, such as a commitment to social justice or political reform, are gray areas. You are not, for example, responsible for an entire political movement on your own. That is outside of your area of responsibility. Nevertheless, it is important to keep in mind that the more power you have, the more your choices may systemically come at the cost of others' boundaries and needs—which means you carry more responsibility to challenge these systems. In a scenario like this one, you're tasked with your corner of that collective work. You're responsible for making decisions that are in alignment with your values and beliefs. These decisions include investing in what you believe in with your precious resources—your time, energy, money, and attention. Those decisions are within your area of personal responsibility and impact.

THIS MIGHT LOOK LIKE . . .

If you're at the self-responsibility stage, this might look like choosing one thing to stop taking responsibility for.

If you're at the self-care stage, this might look like getting curious about where you routinely overdeliver or take responsibility for something that is not yours and making the decision to practice not overextending yourself any longer.

If you're at the self-trust stage, this might look like slowing down to notice how your capacity expands when you create boundaries between what is and is not your responsibility. Isn't it amazing how much more energy you have when you are no longer trespassing your boundaries and overserving?

If you're at the self-love stage, this might look like taking a deep breath and coming to terms with WHY you're overinvolving yourself to begin with by unearthing the roots of this pattern of trying to control the uncontrollable. How has it served you? How might you support yourself in no longer participating in this pattern?

If you're at the advocacy stage, this might look like having a conversation with a friend, relative, or coworker to set boundaries and no longer take on things you have determined aren't your personal responsibility.

You Do Not Need $20,000 or Six Weeks of Paid Vacation to Feel Satisfied with Your Life

When I was a child, I remember watching my sister through the open door of her bedroom as she stacked her pennies up one by one. She had a cigar box that she kept all of her "monies" in, and every day she would pull out the collection of coins and begin stacking them by kind. Then she would write the amount on a piece of paper and put the box away.

As a child her wealth accumulation was slow. A dime found under the couch. A quarter on the ground while walking to the playground. A fistful of pennies in an Easter egg. Fifty cents from the tooth fairy.

She was patient, biding her time as she amassed her small fortune.

This is an approach I encourage you to take with sustenance.

Too often, we withhold satisfaction from ourselves because we are laboring under the belief that a change needs to be big or flashy to have an impact on our lives. In believing this, we overlook the dozens of opportunities we have every day to turn toward ourselves and make choices that prioritize our personal preferences.

If you allow it, the moments that sustain you are pulled from the corners of your life, salvaged moments piled one upon another. You don't need $20,000 or six weeks of paid vacation. Your sustenance will be accumulated one reclaimed moment, choice, or opportunity at a time. Begin with one intentional moment. Stack it upon another. Add them up, one by one. Be patient with yourself as you accumulate your moments of satisfaction. Take heart in each second spent feeding yourself what you are truly hungry for.

Commitments to My Need for Sustenance

— Everything I do is in service to meeting my needs, including how I seek sustenance. Meeting my need for sustenance is about feeding myself what I'm really hungry for physically and energetically rather than settling for what does not satisfy me.

— I might have a habit of waiting until I'm in crisis to start meeting my sustenance needs. This can feel absolutely exhilarating—but it's unsustainable. I will burn out.

— If I do have this habit, it's important to get a sense of my warning signs. What starts happening in myself and my life when I put my needs off for too long? The more awareness I have here, the better I can care for myself.

— Gratitude and sustenance are deeply linked. It's time to start appreciating myself for what I *have* done rather than waiting until I've "done enough" or until someone else acknowledges my efforts. This is an essential capacity-builder.

— Do what is doable. It can be small. It can be "silly." It can be incredibly basic. It all matters.

CHAPTER 5

Trust

BLESSING

I trust myself because I am committed to knowing myself.

I have taken the time to familiarize myself with my inner workings. I have sat beside my fears and curled up into my own lap during times of grief. I take care to attend to the places in my mental, emotional, physical, and spiritual bodies where I am worn thin from use, where I have been systematically disempowered, and where I carry my hurt.

Each day I make the conscious choice to feel into the spaciousness of trust instead of worshiping at the mountain of my inadequacy. I stand in the awe of possibility and know that there is a certain chaos to getting my bearings here. I may knock down everything in my inner landscape as I experiment. I may have to pause, take stock, and start at the beginning again a million times. I am willing to generously give myself whatever I require to nurture my capacity to stay here, faithful in my discomfort.

I will never get it right all of the time. I will fail many times before I figure it out. Trust is not built through success but in the moments surrounding a perceived failure. It is cultivated or lost based on how I speak to myself and about myself during these moments. My failure doesn't say a single thing about my readiness. Failure is how I grow.

I earn my own trust through the consistency of my own attention. Caring for myself means staying by my side, whether or not I take action, whether or not I follow through or show up for myself in the way I might like.

"BUT . . ." I WHISPERED, "what if I start showing up as I am, and there is no one who still loves me on the other side?" I could barely get the words out. This profound risk of loss was what stopped me every single time, because underneath it all, no matter how hard I've worked to heal myself from it, I carry a core wound that who I am innately is not worthy of love. I did not trust that someone would be there for me if I allowed my true self to come through.

Over the years, I created so many shields to protect that wound. The constant thrum of my perfectionism. The overachieving. Saying yes when I desperately wanted to say no. The choke hold of people-pleasing my way into relationships, rooted in the belief that my relationships were dependent on making myself as easy as possible to be around. I did not trust that the world would like my fullest expression of myself.

I was unbearably restless inside the small box I kept myself in, but the only thing scarier than having to stay there forever was venturing out, only to be abandoned by the people I had surrounded myself with. The risk of loss felt insurmountable. It didn't matter how many therapists or loved ones told me that my life *would, in fact, be better* once I embraced my true nature and welcomed my full expression. I felt incapacitated when confronted with my own messiness and preoccupied with standing guard outside of that core wound.

You might be there too. But know this: your primary relationship in your life, from the day you are born until the day you die, is your relationship with yourself. The more of yourself you welcome into your life, the more intact and trustworthy that relationship will be. You can be scared, but that doesn't mean that you aren't ready to let yourself out of that little box.

How We Lose Trust

Trust is created when you can count on someone to show up in a caring and steadfast manner over the course of your relationship. We yearn for the consistency of trust, and yet many of us lose connection with it, both through big, painful moments and the insidious buildup of subtle moments over time. We may be able to easily pinpoint large breaches of trust but unable to pinpoint the small ways our trust in ourselves and others is undermined on a daily basis—through action, inaction, cruel words, and refusals to witness the fullness of our existence. Unlike grandiose turning points or epiphanies, these moments are often small repetitive acts that diminish our ability to trust ourselves over time.

When I was young, I had a basketball coach who led our team by yelling, breaking us down into pieces in an attempt to make us trust her more than we trusted ourselves. I remember looking around the court and noticing that this type of coaching did work for some of the girls on my team. They were inspired by the force of her honesty. They ran faster. They played better. But this style of coaching had a different effect on me. Instead of lighting me up, it shut me down.

"Mara! I told you already, do NOT dribble the ball. Pass or shoot. Those are your only options." My coach yelled from the sidelines as I attempted to dribble the ball past midcourt during a scrimmage at practice one afternoon. I hadn't been paying attention. I didn't remember what she had told me. I acted without thinking. I unconsciously trusted my instinct. In this moment of reprimand, I could feel myself shrinking under the weight of everything I was supposed to remember.

The message here was simple:

Override your natural impulse. Do what I
tell you to do. Make up for your flaws.

The truth is I wasn't a strong dribbler. Clumsy since birth, I had developed a habit of watching my feet instead of watching ahead of me for the next move or opponent. I watched my feet so that I wouldn't trip on my shoelaces while playing, fall down a hill when walking through the woods, or trip going up the stairs, all of which happened to me regularly. But when dribbling up the court, watching one's feet is a disadvantage. We were only teenagers, but my coach was competitive. My dribbling was a liability, and her solution was to keep me from dribbling at all because the outcome of winning was more important than my growth as a player or my experience of the game.

These are the kinds of incidents that undermine our relationships with ourselves. One reprimand. One redirection. In and of itself, this relationship with my basketball coach might have been meaningless, but it was one example of **many** over the course of my life. With time, these reprimands built up inside of me, reinforcing a belief that I didn't know what was best and that seeking success meant looking outside myself for direction and approval. During the three years of working with this coach, I eventually forgot dribbling was an option available to me. With the repetition of the reprimand, I heard it more and more as a universal truth instead of my coach's opinion. With the repetition of the reprimand, I incorporated it into my understanding of myself.

I am a person who cannot dribble.

When I get the ball, I must pass or shoot.

This loss of trust in ourselves manifests as a deeply held knowing that who and how we are is not important in our interpersonal relationships or the larger systems we operate within. Similarly, when we ignore and override our own needs, desires, and ideas in order to belong and seek external validation, we learn that our tender humanity comes second to maintaining the status quo. We are taught and in turn teach ourselves that who and how we are is not as important or worthy as what we do, how quickly we do it, and how well we play our designated or chosen roles in our families, communities, workplaces, relationships, and society.

Many of us are afraid to act intuitively or to grant ourselves permission readily because of a deep and pervasive lack of trust in our inner voice and our ability to know ourselves and make the right decision on our own behalf. We are conditioned to trust in things we sense are steady, reliable, and immovable—and we experience our own messy, fumbling ineptitude as evidence we are untrustworthy rather than evidence of our shared humanity.

We have been taught that if left to our own devices we would consume every last crumb in our house, fail to begin the project in our hearts, or never get up off the couch. If we existed without the steady confines of a diet or a plan, we would be in a lawless state of gluttony, inaction, and indecision. We have been taught the lie that without a rigid structure or guru to follow, we cannot make our own decisions or take action to create the lives that we want. We have been taught that if no one were telling us to stop or to start, we never would. That some bodies are worthier than other bodies because of the color of their skin, their size, sexual orientation, ability, age, or gender identity. That worth has to be earned through active participation in systems that discriminate against us. That without the strictness demanding we lose weight or run the marathon or simply get out of bed in the morning, we would somehow self-destruct.

Or we have been so terrified of failure that we set out on a path where we are hell-bent on not becoming like those people. *Those people.* The ones without any self-control. The ones who lack willpower. The ones who are lazy and slovenly. The ones who will never make anything of themselves. The ones whom no one loves. We are scared that without the structure imposed on us, we might find out that deep inside of ourselves, one of *those people* is hiding in our own skin.

It is important to examine and understand that we lose trust through both personal experiences and the impact of continually interacting with systems that discriminate against humans who fall outside the societal ideal. It is essential to attend to differences when talking about trust because we are impacted by the world's continued reaction to us based on our intersection of identities. This treatment informs our reality, self-image, and sense of what is possible for our lives. We cannot relate to one another or rebuild a positive and trustworthy relationship with ourselves if we don't take the time to understand or take responsibility for our privilege and/or the impact that structural oppression has had on how we are conditioned to know ourselves.

Healing from this loss of self-trust requires our active participation as we become devoted to asking, "Whom does this thought belong to? Who is benefitting from me seeing myself or the possibilities for my life this way?" It can be challenging to heal from a loss of trust because we may have learned to mistrust our instincts, inner voice, unique ways of doing things, or perspective. As you are healing, your inner

voice might initially feel like a loud mishmash of the voices and opinions you accumulated over your life, well-worn pathways that with
time have come to define you and your understanding of yourself. In
such a scenario, some self-help leaders might tell you you'll know your
true voice because it is kind or loving, but society's programming is
too insidious to be taken lightly. It crawls inside of you and replicates,
until it sounds devastatingly familiar—a ubiquitous "truth" that everyone, everywhere agrees that you need to conform to or else. If this is
your experience, be gentle with yourself and get curious about these
communications. Understand that there might be hurt or traumatized
parts of you that speak urgently and violently in an attempt to protect you from a perceived threat. Understand that even when these
messages are not the whole of you, at this point they might make up a
dominant part of your self-talk. Question these narratives as they arise,
holding true to your intention not only to know yourself but also to
learn to communicate with yourself in a new way, one that enables you
to feel safe and held in your inner landscape.

Journal prompts to dive deeper:

What does trust mean to you?

What are some physical, behavioral, or emotional signs that
you are experiencing trust?

What are some physical, behavioral, or emotional signs that
you are not experiencing trust?

When did you learn it wasn't safe to trust yourself?

Over the course of your life, what promise to yourself have
you routinely not kept?

What is the cost of not believing you will keep the promises
you make to yourself?

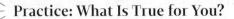

Practice: What Is True for You?

How do you start to rebuild trust with yourself? By getting a sense of your own opinions, desires, interests, needs, and wants.

Fifteen years ago I was standing in front of a huge display of socks at TJ Maxx. I had stopped there because that morning I had been combing through my sock drawer, frustrated and unimpressed that I didn't own enough socks, and I didn't even like the socks I did own. As I stood there in front of the huge display, I was gobsmacked by the realization I had never really stopped to think about what kinds of socks I liked. I had acquired socks from my grandparents at Christmas when I was in college. I had stolen socks from my sisters when they stayed at my house or from my partner when I was rushing out of the house in the morning. I had acquired my socks mostly by accident for the entirety of my life.

Standing there, I realized I hadn't been paying attention to many parts of my life and had instead allowed things to happen *to* me. I felt myself swimming in overwhelm as I realized my lack of participation extended to so many areas of my life: food, work, daily schedule, sex, getting dressed in the morning, choosing activities to do with myself. How long had I been living on autopilot? What did I want? What did I like?

Up until that point in my life, each decision had required the arduous process of gathering other people's opinions and seeking out experts in the field. Things either seemed to "just happen" to me, or they were the result of thousands of hours of scouring the Internet for an expert to tell me the *right* and *best* thing to do, looking in vain for an answer everyone in the world would agree with.

I did not consider connecting with my own truth or acting from a place of personal sovereignty. I operated from the hope that I could do things in a way that would earn me maximum external approval. And of course, when you're in a state like that, it's impossible to trust your own truth because your goodness, safety, and belonging are predicated on silencing yourself and attempting to please everyone around you.

But the truth is, with practice you *can* trust your body, mind, and spirit to give you vital information about how to proceed. Trust doesn't require our perfection but it does require our presence. It requires you to choose to stand in front of the display of socks and patiently figure out which one feels right to YOU. It requires the willingness to be wrong for the sake of getting to know yourself. It requires the willingness to go through the effort of returning the socks and trying another pair.

As you stand in front of this theoretical sock display, you are in a moment of opportunity. You can choose not to abandon yourself, even in your discomfort or awkwardness. You strengthen your capacity for being in a relationship with yourself each moment you remain, each moment you stay open to your feelings and what you really want. You bolster your self-trust with your next decision, open to the possibility of making a choice and it not being the right one. This is trust not only to make decisions on your own behalf but also to navigate the fallout of an "unsuccessful" choice.

START HERE

Pull out your journal and ask yourself, *What is true for me today?*
You.
Not your coworker. Or partner. Or mother. Or the media. Not your best friend.
Or what you've learned is expected of you.
You.
Ask yourself once a day.
Start where you are at this moment. Don't overthink it.
Allow space and time for your answers to reveal themselves. You may find that what is true for you right now is something subtle or insignificant. After your first few answers, you might unearth a big and deeper truth that you aren't ready to approach. Whatever comes up, let it be true.

Give it permission to exist. Utter it aloud. Tell a confidant or write about it in your journal. Bring it to your next therapy session. Hold it in gentle hands, without censorship, self-judgment, or ridicule. Honoring what is true for you doesn't mean you have to rush into truth-inspired action. It is enough to explore it on your own, in the privacy of your own mind. With time, as you learn to be forthcoming with yourself, you will be better able to determine which truths are ripe for forward movement and which require a little bit more time and stamina to prepare themselves within you. You do not have to rush yourself. Rebuilding trust is good work, and it takes time.

THIS MIGHT LOOK LIKE . . .

If you're at the self-responsibility stage, this might look like "simply" acknowledging your truth, giving it permission to exist, uttering it aloud, and gaining familiarity with it.

If you're at the self-care stage, this might look like checking in with yourself throughout the day whenever you are presented with a decision, both large and small, to see what feels best to YOU, before you check in with anyone else.

If you're at the self-trust stage, this might look like increased comfort from knowing your own mind and trusting in your ability to remain by your own side no matter the outcome of your decisions.

If you're at the self-love stage, this might look like relishing finding new corners of your life to imbue with truth that bring you into greater alignment with what lights you up and makes you tick.

If you're at the advocacy stage, this might look like sharing your truth with someone in your life who is safe to share with. Invite reflection and conversation. Explore the truth together, looking at it from new angles.

Healing a Loss of Trust

Lucy couldn't remember a time in her childhood when either of her parents asked her what she was thinking or feeling. They expected her to do what she was asked, in accordance with their timeline. She remembered feeling afraid of her dad even though she didn't remember any distinct experiences of abuse, but she was terrified that "something bad would happen" if she didn't do what was expected of her. She could never put her finger on what that bad thing was exactly, but she knew she had never wanted to find out. When Lucy and I started working together she was fifty-two. Her children were grown, and her marriage was dissolving. She wanted to feel confident in the face of these shifting realities, but she felt disconnected from herself—so disconnected, in fact, that she often wondered aloud if she had ever *been* connected to begin with. Lucy was an expert on what other people thought she should do, want, and become. She knew what her mother had wanted for her, what her father thought was foolish, and what her soon-to-be ex-husband couldn't stand about her.

But Lucy had no idea what **she** wanted until she began to get curious about what was true for her. This started in small ways—what she really thought about a proposed family get-together, whether she wanted to pick up more hours at work that week, or what she wanted to eat for dinner now that there was no one else to prepare food for. It felt ridiculous, audacious even, to ask these questions, but with time, she came to know herself better. She knew her own mind. By asking herself, *Whose voice is that?* she was more easily able to distinguish her inner voice from the voices of the people who surrounded her, the voices she had defaulted her decision-making to for so long. With time she realized that what she wanted was to start volunteering on Sunday mornings instead of going to church, to cancel her cable subscription, and to eat peanut-butter-and-jelly sandwiches for dinner. She was surprised to notice that as she incorporated more of her own truths into her life, she trusted herself more. She felt capable of making a decision on her own behalf, possibly for the first time in her life. It wasn't like a light switched on though. It was the awkward fumbling of learning how to walk again, lurching forward and misspeaking or falling back into a familiar pattern of overcommitting and later going back to correct herself.

No matter how you cared for yourself before this moment, true tending is possible for you. No matter what you've done or who you've been, you are allowed to rebuild your self-trust. No matter how disconnected from it you might feel, your truth, your inner wisdom, and your self-trust will never disappear completely. A spark of it can always be recovered. Each breath and moment are an opportunity to rebuild your relationship with yourself.

The model we are collectively taught is to fumble along, buying all the quick fixes and listening to the experts, until we have an epiphany, and suddenly everything magically clicks into place. In this figment of imagination, our self-care is suddenly easy. We adeptly hold healthy boundaries without making anyone around us upset. We don't struggle to prioritize our own care anymore and deftly life-hack our calendars with the care we require without disturbing any external commitments. We are able to show up for ourselves in deep and meaningful ways without upending the status quo in our lives.

This is a beautiful, seductive myth, but it is just that—a myth. Waiting until things suddenly click and feel easy is why so many of us have unmet needs. I disagree with the idea that a magical epiphany is going to make having a trustworthy relationship with ourselves effortless and easy. Beyond the fantasy, the problem with this narrative is that it has nothing to do with how humans actually build loving relationships. Rebuilding self-trust is a relational act. We rebuild trust when we take radical responsibility for our needs and own what is ours to own. We rebuild trust when we refuse to abandon ourselves even when we are profoundly disappointed. We rebuild trust by taking our choices off autopilot so that we can make each choice standing in this moment, in this body, in this place in time and ask ourselves, "What do I want? What do I need? What's best for me right now?"

The reason you don't trust yourself is not because you are a personal failure but because the world is filled with people who benefit from you not trusting yourself. Capitalism, structural oppression, White supremacy, patriarchy, the diet industry—these are all systems set up to suppress your authentic connection with yourself. For those of us who have trespassed against ourselves for a long period of time, it is a big shift to go from hoping we will find an external solution to taking responsibility for ourselves and standing in our own sovereignty, as we fine-tune our energetic alignment and build self-trust. There may be many good reasons for your lack of self-trust, but healing your relationship with yourself and taking action in your life from this moment on are your responsibility.

The first three chapters of this book have spoken to you about taking radical responsibility for your body and life through safety, rest, and sustenance. That work was already in service to rebuilding a trusting relationship with yourself, a trust built on turning to yourself and tuning in to your feelings and needs. These acts of befriending the human, inconvenient, messy, and complicated parts of yourself are the bedrock self-trust is built upon. It is through these small acts that you remind yourself you are a person who matters, a person who is real and lovable even with all your perceived flaws.

The consistency of this connection with yourself is what is trustworthy, not the individual acts themselves. While the acts are great, the strength of the self-trust you are rebuilding lies even deeper, in the connection you are forming with yourself and the familiarity you are gaining with your inner wilderness.

Journal prompts to dive deeper:

Over the course of your life, who has benefited from you not trusting yourself?

What thoughts and feelings arise when you consider actively working to rebuild your self-trust?

What grief do you carry around self-trust?

What have you been avoiding that you know you need to take a look at? (And what do you need to be able to do it in a way that is sustainable and kind?)

What do you imagine real self-trust might look or feel like?

Practice: Affirming Self-Talk and Sowing Seeds of Trust

If you have spent your life losing or compromising your own trust, it is your job and privilege to spend the rest of your life earning that trust back.

Telling yourself the truth is the key to rebuilding trust, but it is not the only component. Trust requires truth, yes, but truth ALSO requires trust, and it is unlikely you will be willing to be honest with yourself or comfortable if you haven't addressed your harmful or abusive self-talk. Rebuilding self-trust requires creating an inner ecosystem where truth and trust coexist and where we are willing to confront our own harsh treatment of burgeoning truths. Many of us were conditioned to be unkind to ourselves in the name of growth or reaching our own potential. We are taught to be suspicious of the soft animal of our bodies because our humanity is as unpredictable and inconvenient as it is glorious and true. We are taught that self-acceptance leads to stagnation and that if we were to accept ourselves, we might never amount to anything.

You can't rebuild trust with those tools. Instead, you must practice carving out space for your truth and take responsibility for creating the conditions for that truth to thrive. This requires prioritizing connection with yourself, setting boundaries that protect this connection, and tending to the language you routinely use to speak to yourself.

What do you do when you let yourself down? Is your self-trust ruined if you aren't able to follow through perfectly? No. More important than how or when you take action is how you TALK to yourself about the action you take. Are you approaching yourself with curiosity? Are you communicating with yourself about why you weren't able to follow through? What got in the way? How might you need to approach the task differently to have a greater sense of success? What would it be like to stay and work with yourself instead of abandoning yourself at the merest whiff of failure?

The reason you're not following through with your promises to yourself is not that there's something wrong with you, you can't hack it, or you just didn't get the special "tending" gene that the rest of us got. *You aren't broken.* There is nothing wrong with you. You haven't been following through with your promises to yourself for very real reasons—reasons that are personal and unique to you and have little to do with your willpower or ability to create change in your life. You might not be following through because you chose a goal you think you *should* pursue, but if you're really honest with yourself, you aren't invested in that goal. You might be telling yourself there is only one *right* way to go about what you are trying to do, but that way is not a good fit for your style of getting things done. You might feel disempowered, afraid, and disconnected from your wise, intuitive self because your conditioning has contaminated your self-image. You might need additional support to make good on a goal you chose for yourself.

Your expectations of yourself might be riddled with perfectionism, and you might be telling yourself something isn't worth doing if you aren't able to do it perfectly the very first time. Holding yourself to a standard you are never going to be able to meet is abusive to yourself. There might be many utterly valid reasons for not feeling ready to take action in your life, AND as the tender steward of your life, you still get to choose what you'd like to do. These are the types of conversations that are integral to creating and maintaining a healthy and trustworthy relationship with yourself.

AN EXAMPLE OF WHAT THIS MIGHT LOOK LIKE:

Let's say that I want to start writing again. I've done my due diligence honoring this desire. I have worked hard to reclaim creativity from my years and years of conditioning within a toxic productivity culture where I didn't feel I had permission to prioritize something unless it produced a tangible result. I have made the aim obtainable by keeping my promise to myself as simple and sustainable as possible. I am making an effort to be kind to myself through this process, knowing I struggle with carving out space to do things that don't feel absolutely necessary when I have a massive to-do list.

It goes great for a couple of days, but then I notice I'm starting to avoid it. This avoidance isn't overt; instead, I'm subconsciously arranging and filling my day so that writing is pushed to the bottom of my very long list. I'm writing with less and less frequency, until I stop showing up for my initial desire completely.

Historically, this is where I jump in to beat myself up, telling myself I am a failure and will always be a failure. I would abuse myself by making my inaction mean I can't trust myself to follow through on even the simplest task. My lack of stamina and willpower are embarrassing. I am too weak to do something that everyone else on the planet seems to easily handle. Historically, I would have made myself feel so ashamed that I would be spurred back to action—not because I felt empowered or supported but because I was willing to bypass my own discomfort to keep myself safe from future abuse. **This is not a sustainable approach to taking action in your life.** It may work for a time. It may feel effective. You may have been taught that this is how *everyone* takes action in their lives, but that is not true. You do not have to beat yourself up to give yourself permission to begin again. You do not need to do things perfectly for them to be worthy pursuits.

What if instead I approached myself saying: *Hey, what gives? I've noticed that you haven't followed through with that thing you said you really wanted to make happen in your life. What do you think is going on? Is there something you need for the process to be easier—a tool, a support system, or a piece of information you don't have? Are you feeling scared? What are you scared of? Can I listen to what is coming up for you? Can I give you permission to be the human that you are and not do this perfectly? Can I have your back and support you and make a plan with you? How might you approach this in a way that is sustainable and kind?*

That second approach is one that builds trust. It is one example of how you might communicate with yourself to reconnect with your original desire and get creative about circumventing whatever obstacles are getting in the way of your following through. You WILL make mistakes. You will fail to follow through. You won't get it right. You will have to keep returning to your relationship with yourself, problem-solving and working out a new approach. The way you speak to yourself in these moments will make a profound difference in how your relationship with yourself feels. If you want to be able to trust yourself implicitly and to know your own mind, you cannot overlook the quality of your communication with yourself.

You begin tending to your needs with simple acts—glasses of water and the permission to notice when your breath feels shallow in your throat. You line up your vitamins. You luxuriate in the shower. You turn your face toward the sun when you walk to your car in the morning. You choose to care how things feel instead of diminishing or minimizing the experience of your life. But while you practice mattering, old stories will creep in around the edges. Like weeds, their intricate root systems travel beneath your earth, connecting and persisting even as you track, uproot, and compost individual plants.

Am I allowed just to choose how I feel about myself?

How can I forgive myself for everything I've done wrong?

What if this kindness is a joke or a lie and I am doubly
    disappointed for having believed in it?

At the root of this line of questioning is a fundamental mistrust in your ability to shape and interpret your reality. You weren't taught that you are allowed to decide for yourself what is true for you. You were taught to look outside yourself to verify your perception of reality or to disregard it completely in the name of belonging.

But you are the decision-maker, the personal historian, and the enoughness validator in your life. You get to choose what is true for you. You are allowed to see yourself as an important and valuable person, worthy of the care you ache for. Your choice to approve of yourself fiercely and unconditionally, flaws and all, has nothing to do with anyone else. You do not have to consult anyone. You do not need to get a second opinion. You do not even need to share your choice with anyone else if you don't want to. You get to choose what is true for you. And you rebuild trust one choice and understanding word at a time.

START HERE

Turn your attention to how you speak to yourself when you've disappointed yourself, failed, or dropped the ball.

Ask yourself: *Are these words building self-trust or destroying it?*

If you aren't sure, a good place to start is with how you feel in the conversation with yourself. Do you feel seen, heard, and supported? Do you feel ashamed? Do you feel embarrassed?

Feeling ashamed, unseen, unsupported, or diminished after conversations with yourself is an excellent opportunity to tune in to your thoughts with greater awareness and get curious about how you are speaking to yourself.

Ask yourself: *What am I afraid of? What belief system is activated right now? Who does this thought or belief system belong to? Who is benefitting from my feeling this way?*

Get the photo of your young self that you located in chapter 1. Would you say these words to that child? If not, you don't deserve them either. The words you use to describe yourself become your self-image over time. Choose thoughts and self-descriptors that build self-trust instead of destroying it.

THIS MIGHT LOOK LIKE . . .

If you're at the self-responsibility stage, this might look like paying closer attention to the words, descriptors, beliefs, and meaning-making that move through your inner landscape over the course of the day.

If you're at the self-care stage, this might look like noticing you feel particularly upset or anxious and then walking yourself back to figure out how you're speaking to yourself.

If you're at the self-trust stage, this might look like actively working with comfortable go-to thought patterns that arise during moments of stress and coming up with a plan for approaching yourself differently in the future.

If you're at the self-love stage, this might look like being gentle with yourself when devastatingly familiar thought patterns reveal themselves and then reminding yourself that other narratives and reframes are also available to you.

If you're at the advocacy stage, this might look like reality-testing with the people you feel safest with as you explore your self-talk in relationship. Writer and researcher Brené Brown shares a beautiful prompt for these kinds of conversations: "The story I'm making up is . . ."[1] Using this prompt to describe the story you are telling yourself about a situation enables you to express the voices in your head and to share them with the people around you to explore more readily.

Starting with What You Know

Rebuilding trust doesn't have a thing to do with your perfection, though you may have been taught it does. It doesn't require you to jump through hoops or perform in just the right way to earn it. You don't need anyone else's permission to claim it or to embody every last square inch of your life. You do not need to wait until you've reached a certain milestone for it to be available to you. There is not a complex code you need to spend a lifetime in therapy unraveling to finally begin taking care of yourself.

It might feel as though you don't really know yourself well enough to trust you can care for yourself that way—yet. Your fear of not knowing

EVERYTHING might reinforce a belief that you aren't ready to commit to your tending until you better understand what you need. You might tell yourself you need to learn more skills or figure out the absolute perfect way to go about this to begin. I want to respectfully call bullshit on that—both your complete lack of knowing **and** the idea that we are only ready to take action when we are perfectly able to execute something.

You do not need to trust yourself unconditionally to begin rebuilding trust in small ways. If that is what you are waiting for, you will be waiting for a long time. Instead of waiting until everything is crystal clear and perfectly resolved, start with whatever truth is available to you in this moment, no matter how trivial. You may not know everything, but you do know *something*. This is your invitation to start with what you know. Start with something manageable. You rebuild trust as you slow down to connect with yourself and honor the burgeoning truths as they arise.

> Can you trust yourself to carve out five minutes for your care? What about an afternoon?
>
> Can you trust yourself to wear something a little out of the ordinary that you've been wanting to wear but have been worrying about how it will be received?
>
> Can you trust yourself to make one small (but deliciously well-fitting) decision without asking for any other opinions?
>
> Can you trust yourself to believe that the world will not end if you allow yourself to take up more space in your life, even if only for the next minute or hour?

Start with what feels possible. Be permissive in your exploration. Be kind. And if you get lost, give yourself permission to begin again.

Commitments to My Need for Trust

— Trust happens when I build a legacy of experiences over time. Note: this has absolutely nothing to do with perfection.

— In a moment when I feel terrified to trust myself, I will remind myself that I have been taught to feel this way. I have been taught that if I let my guard down, even just a little bit, I will go wild and self-destruct. I have been taught to outsource my responsibility and abandon myself. However, what I choose to do next is completely up to me.

— Healing my relationship with myself requires active participation, unpacking moments of self-abandonment and recommitting to taking actions in my own best interest.

— A core component of this is knowing what is true for me right now. This is a deepening of that self-responsibility. I decide what's true. Not what someone else says, likes, or wants. Me. Trust and truth go hand in hand.

— I can't bully myself into trust and healing. Start with what I know. Move gently with myself. I can always begin again.

CHAPTER 6

Integrity

BLESSING

I know what I value. I prioritize and align my life with my values as much as possible. I take action from a deeply rooted place of alignment, intentionally cocreating the world I want to live in with each choice I make.

I am cleaning up here, dusting the shelves and getting rid of the stories that no longer serve me. I am preparing for the arrival of the fullest expression of myself the way I would prepare for the arrival of a queen. I am baking a chocolate Bundt cake drizzled with ganache, and I am pulling out the good china.

I honor the grief enmeshed with a lifetime of diminishing myself and holding back. I am breaking free from my perfectionism, wading through the thick murkiness of discomfort as I stand before you with everything I have to offer, knowing fully I will never live up to the ideal self who lives in my mind. I am nourishing the bravery required to bring the fullest version of myself to every day of the rest of my life.

I am reclaiming the energy I once exclusively spent trying to keep others comfortable. I am using that energy to feed my own pleasure. I am best equipped for this pursuit because I know myself better than anyone else on this planet knows me. I am uniquely positioned to pad around this internal terrain, turning over rocks and raking my hands through the earth to gently locate places where I might be overserving, overdelivering, and taking care of others at the expense of my own needs. I am watering my inner landscape and pruning the dead leaves to divert energy to new growth. I am both focused and playful here, knowing I am allowed to pace myself. I am allowed to prioritize and feed my pleasure, and doing so enhances my capacity to make aligned, intentional choices moving forward.

I ask myself: Where am I carrying more than my fair share of a burden? What am I shouldering that does not belong to me? What am I avoiding because I am uncomfortable or feel unprepared?

There is stickiness here as I confront patterns fastened in place since I was a child. A pattern of eating things, of swallowing other people's pain as if it were my own and wearing it on my body as if my helpful compliance could save me from scrutiny or rejection. A pattern of shape-shifting, of being who I think you want me to be instead of who I am, a distorting game of telephone without any winners. A pattern of hiding until I somehow magically have the right words, all the while grieving the knowledge that I will never have the right words. A pattern of becoming a living, breathing apology for the things that were not my responsibility to hold but that I carried all the same. A pattern of holding up false responsibilities and being too exhausted to nourish the things that I actually value.

I remind myself that these patterns are in me, but they are not me. I am whole, distinct, and autonomous. I am separate from my family of origin, even as we share emotional space and physical resources. I am separate from my partner and from my children. This separateness does not isolate me. I am not lonely here because it is here where I can truly be with myself. I belong to myself first. My first responsibility is to my own existence, pouring my energy into creating a life that is in alignment with my values.

My hand is on my heart, pledging allegiance to my own thriving.

I ask myself:

What have I been waiting for?

What would I do differently if this moment were all I had?

What would I reject or refuse to consume?

What rage would I permit?

What knowing would I embody?

What would I say if I could say anything?

IT WASN'T UNTIL I STARTED TRYING to get pregnant that I truly began to understand the complex functions my organs undertake each day. I was struck by how much of my life I had spent obsessed with judging my body for how it looked and how others perceived me, yet how little of my life I had spent in absolute wonderment at the fact that all the while I was judging it, forcing it through diet after diet, and punishing it with merciless exercise routines, my body was moving through a symphony of functions each day.

My body was working to support me, even as I was treating it so unfairly.

Propped up by lessons learned in health class about the profound dangers of teen pregnancy, I expected to get pregnant easily. I did not get pregnant easily. Instead, this path included many attempts, doctors, sperm donors, supplements, and months of acupuncture.

During this time, I developed a profound respect for my body, provoking an entirely new relationship with self-care. Instead of the familiar, well-worn concept of self-care as a tool for betterment, it became a conversation with my organs, cells, skin, blood, and digestion. Instead of a tool to make me thinner, smarter, more productive, or patient, this new understanding of self-support was one with a much deeper why.

Wanting my body or productivity to be better was a thinly veiled grasp at more secure attachment and belonging. I reasoned that if I could make myself better, no one would reject or abandon me. But in all of that betterment, I routinely rejected and abandoned myself.

Though my curiosity and fascination with my body have grown over the last five years, what has been most compelling is how deeply rooted my relationship has become in my values of sustainability, humanity, justice, and intentional, cyclical living.

The care I work to offer myself mirrors the care I work toward for all of us and for the planet, which is not to say this is comfortable. There can be so much grief interwoven in holding myself accountable to these values when my toxic productivity or diet mentality want me to rush past or abandon myself during fallow periods of growth. I would be out of integrity if I didn't extend kind permission to myself, however uncomfortable it may be to do so.

What Is Integrity?

Your body, life, and energy are for you to enjoy and use as you see fit. You do not have to give it all away to be deemed good by others or to earn love. Being in integrity requires being true to yourself and honest and upright in your experiences with others. This requires knowing yourself and your values, the outer limits of your capacity, and how to use your precious resources with a greater sense of purpose and alignment.

Developing integrity requires honesty because it is impossible to be honest with others unless you are first honest with yourself. It requires self-awareness, as you cannot accurately communicate what you do not know. It requires the knowledge and patience to locate yourself within systems of oppression that have handed you false versions of yourself, reinforced by the repetition of experiences from birth through adulthood as well as those passed down through generations. It requires the vulnerability of being in right relationship with your community, bringing unfinished parts of yourself to the world around you, and being open to feedback from humans you trust. It requires you to normalize the inner transformation you experience as you integrate and allow yourself to be changed by new information. It requires an openness to the discomfort that comes hand in hand with growth.

Coming into alignment is the practice of devoting yourself to yourself and the world you long to cocreate with each decision. It is the choice to turn toward yourself a little bit more in each moment. Each decision throughout your day is an invitation to show up in the world with greater integrity—from what you have for breakfast, to what you say yes to, to what you say no to, to what you take personally, and to what you really claim responsibility for.

When you are out of alignment, everything in your life feels challenging. You wonder why things just aren't as easy for you as they are for everyone else. When it comes to showing up in your life with care, attention, and intention, you feel as though no matter what you try, nothing is working. You feel frustrated with how long it's taking, blaming yourself for not being able to deliver on command. You ache for a greater purpose as you trudge through your days, frustrated by your lack of connection and divine contribution. You feel disconnected from your body and inner world, believing self-connection is a privilege for someone with more time, money, or access than you have.

To be clear, I am not blaming you for this. We are sold this disconnection from the day we are born. We may have been raised by humans who were unable because of circumstance, history, or lack of skill to model this deep connection for us when we were children. We certainly have been raised within systems set up to benefit from our lack of self-trust and self-love. We carry within us legacies of this conditioning, of feeling othered and forced to work just that much harder to prove our worth and keep ourselves safe.

This disconnection is not your fault, but reconnection is your responsibility. Honoring the presence and power of your needs and desires is your responsibility, even before you are equipped to meet them. Divesting from systems of oppression in whatever way you can through education and connection with a community that raises you up and affirms your inherent worthiness is your responsibility.

Journal prompts to dive deeper:

Where are you out of alignment with what matters to you most?

What is important to you that feels impossible to prioritize?

What rules do you live by each day that feel supportive?

What rules do you live by each day that aren't in alignment for you or aren't in alignment for you any longer?

If you had a magic wand and could TRULY choose how to spend your time, attention, energy, and money—what would you prioritize?

If you had a magic wand and could TRULY choose how to spend your time, attention, energy, and money—what would you minimize or stop prioritizing?

Practice: Defining Your Priorities

How do you want to live? Does the way you want to live reflect what you care about? Does the way you want to live reflect your values? What have you been preoccupied with that you don't want to be preoccupied with anymore? Do your daily actions reflect your priorities?

These are the questions that are essential to meeting your needs for integrity, sustainable contribution, and right timing. Though it might feel like this practice will enable you to be more productive—and that might happen as a by-product—that's not what it's about. This is a practice in gaining essential clarity around using your energy in a way that aligns with the vision for the world you want to cocreate with your actions, that enables you to contribute in a way that feels cohesive and connected.

You cannot do, BE, or prioritize everything. (I know, I hate it too.) But your willingness to be decisive about what matters to you most creates a positive-integrity feedback loop as you start bringing those projects to completion. Each time you accomplish something, you increase the evidence that you *can* do things. You *can* complete things. You *can* trust yourself to follow through.

Without this necessary clarity, you might find you lack forward momentum in your life, and you might mistakenly attribute that lack of momentum to your own personal failing. However, spreading yourself thin by overcommitting and shouldering the belief that you can and should be able to accomplish all things at all times creates an ecosystem of burnout. It is disempowering to have your energy pulled in a multitude of directions and never feel like you are gaining any traction on your projects.

Here's your permission slip: You get to be who and how you are. You get to want what you want. You get to need what you need. None of this has to make sense to anyone else but you. You are your own responsibility. Continually placing yourself at the bottom of your list is an abdication of your tender stewardship.

START HERE

Pull out a big piece of paper and spend ten minutes making a list for each of the following prompts: *What do I want to create, do, or make happen in my life right now? What do I need to take care of?*

Then pull out a different colored pen and narrow each list by asking the following questions: *Do I really want this thing, or do I think I should want it? Maybe I once wanted this thing, but do I still want it?*

These questions seek to narrow your list down to what is truly essential and timely for you at this moment. There may be things on this list that you want to attend to in the future or things you've been lugging around with you from to-do lists in previous years, which you silently judge yourself for never getting done. For this exercise to work, you have to get clear on what is present for you. Know that this list can provide a safe resting place for ideas you aren't ready for, aren't currently interested in, or don't currently have the capacity for.

Once you've done this, circle your top three priorities from both lists, and then claim your number one priority. Be willing to kill your darlings here, or at least push them to the side for the moment. You can always choose fresh priorities once you take action on your first one.

What's next? Commit to taking action in a way that is sustainable, kind, pleasurable, and in integrity for you. Take your priority and break it down into as many manageable steps as possible—tasks that can be done in twenty to thirty minutes or less. These steps will be much easier to put on your to-do list than "working on [WHOLE PRIORITY]", I promise. Be creative as you outline these steps. One of the primary reasons we resist taking action on the things that matter to us is that we carry a narrow scope for how we think we must approach it. There are no rules here. Use the data you've gathered about how you work best and what lights you up to infuse the process of taking action on your priority with a fresh perspective. Then pull out your calendar for the week ahead and schedule one of those action steps.

THIS MIGHT LOOK LIKE . . .

If you're at the self-responsibility stage, this might look like realizing you've been routinely overcommitting yourself and subsequently blaming yourself for never getting anything done. (Yikes!)

If you're at the self-care stage, this might look like an increased understanding of what YOU need to make good on some of these commitments.

If you're at the self-trust stage, this might look like doing dramatically less because you trust yourself to get to the things on your list in the right timing for you, even when you are frustrated or grief-stricken because you aren't able to move faster.

If you're at the self-love stage, this might look like celebrating yourself during the process because you already know you will eventually bring those projects and priorities to glorious completion.

If you're at the advocacy stage, this might look like working through this process collaboratively with your partner(s), family members, or coworkers to create a map of shared priorities. Spend time bringing everything you individually carry to the table, choose a priority by desire or necessity, and delve deep into who will take responsibility for which part of the process.

The Inexplicable Discomfort of Living a Life Made for Someone Else

I turned over in bed, my eyes swollen from crying all night. A mountain of tissues covered my phone, spilling to the floor when I silenced my alarm. I felt horrible. I had been ignoring the signs of my unhappiness for months. I had been attempting to smooth my fears over and make them behave, afraid that if I changed one thing in my life to make it better, everything would tumble to the ground in a mess. But I could no longer continue living the way I had been, pushing all my needs aside. *I can't keep doing this,* I told myself. *This is so painful.*

If this were the last year of my life,
what would I do differently?

I wouldn't become a social worker. That was the truth I couldn't avoid any longer. I had spent the last four months trying to control the panic I felt every time I thought about completing my graduate program and getting a job in my chosen field. It felt like I was drowning every time I imagined my schedule filling up, my daily employment usurping every last moment of peace and ease that I clung to.

As a second-year social-work student, I was surrounded by burnout. My professors would laugh, making light of their lack of self-care and huge client lists. Secretly, I knew I was pursuing this career because I was good at it, not because I loved it. My professors liked me. I got good grades. I did well in my internships. I was able to build rapport with my clients. I was pursuing this because that was how I had always done things—work as hard as I could to prove myself, put everything else on the back burner, thrive in the presence of praise, and make a plan to move forward based on what other people told me was the right next move. I was pursuing this because I had already chosen it. I had already borrowed hundreds of thousands of dollars in student loans. I had already said yes, and I prided myself on being a person who followed through with their obligations.

For months I had been silencing my truths the minute they bubbled up, wanting to want something other than what I wanted. I tried as hard as I could to get cozy in the life I had chosen, and yet, I could no longer deny my inner wisdom.

Some of the most powerful words a person can utter are *I can't do this anymore.* Whenever I sat down to look for jobs, I couldn't stop thinking about that one day when I would need to take off for a conference where I'd be speaking about my experiences cultivating self-love—my heart's work—even though that day was months away.

It would have been so easy to belittle that one day, bullying it back into the recesses of my mind, touting its unimportance. But instead, that morning I asked myself, *What would freedom feel like?*

An open calendar. The ability to show up in the world
as I am. A million trips to a million conferences where
I could tell my story to empower others to show up in
the world the way they were. Writing in my kitchen
at 8 a.m. in my pajamas. Time to get outside. Space
to care for my future family. Space to be a human
first. Space I had never allowed myself before.

It seemed irrational to derail my entire life plan for one day off months from now, but it was more than a day off. It was an indicator, warning me that the way I was living was out of alignment, that the life I was creating looked good from the outside but was not sustainable and lacked joy from the inside.

In that moment, beneath the noise of my ego and fear, there was a quiet voice that was steadily becoming my own. Beneath the rubble of what was expected of me and what I had created to meet those expectations were my sovereignty and my desire.

What happens when our needs and deep desires take us in the opposite direction of the beautiful plans we have laid out for ourselves? What happens when we begin coming to terms with the many, many ways we have been suppressing our true nature, believing no one will like or accept us as we are? What if we were allowed to choose for ourselves, making decisions for our own lives based on what feels right and true to us?

Meeting your need for integrity requires standing in your own power and actively participating in your life, instead of wandering through the life society lays out for you. This happens in remarkably small ways each day as we build the emotional muscles necessary to make larger and riskier decisions on our own behalf.

At that moment, I made the decision not to become a social worker, but really I made the decision to follow my own path instead of the beautiful plan I had created based on someone else's model of success. For me, this was a big risk, the biggest I had ever encountered. With the choice to prioritize my desire for freedom, I clashed with my inner good girl, the part of myself that wanted to do everything perfectly. In that moment, I could honestly say I wanted to be free more than I wanted to be perfect. And I wanted a life that felt good more than I wanted just about anything else.

Journal prompts to dive deeper:

What would you do differently in your life if you truly believed you had permission to do what was right and best for you?

What truth(s) have you been avoiding?

What might be the best-case scenario if you were to face that truth?

What might be the worst-case scenario if you were to face that truth?

What have you been afraid to say—to yourself or someone else—that you know you need to say?

What are you ready, able, and willing to look at directly, even as it scares you?

The Boundaries That Free Us

A boundary is a verbal communication or action that honors what you are willing to tolerate and advocates for what you require to exist and thrive in a relationship, including your relationship with yourself. Boundaries create trust with ourselves and with others. They allow others to believe us when we offer something, creating a clean energetic exchange without fear of resentment or retribution. Boundaries are protective and kind facilitators of trust. They allow us to relate openly with ourselves and the people around us. Many of us carry fear around receiving because we've experienced relationships with people who have leaky boundaries, people who offered more than they could give and then punished us for it later. In other words, people who haven't created the boundaries necessary to allow them to give openly, generously, and in ways that are aligned with how much they actually have to offer. We may have learned that boundaries are punitive or painful, but by contrast, when we remain in integrity with ourselves and hold our boundaries, we show ourselves that we are committed to our needs and our care. Through tending to ourselves and learning to receive our own care, we are able to repattern our understanding of what it means to belong to ourselves while also being in relationship with the world around us.

To be clear, a boundary isn't an ultimatum or a demand. It isn't a high wall separating you from the world. Instead, a boundary is how you advocate for your needs and communicate to the world what you are genuinely available for. True boundaries will always serve you and your relationships because you—and your truth—are an essential component of all of your relationships. Not sure where you need to set a boundary in your life? An excellent practice is to look for feelings of anger or resent-ment, both of which are neon signs pointing to a boundary that needs clarification or has been trespassed.

A boundary might come in the form of a verbal communication: "It makes me uncomfortable when you speak about my body that way. If you continue, I am going to walk away." It might come in the form of an action: walking away when someone is speaking about your body in a way that is uncomfortable. Or it might come in the form of space: no longer spending time with the person who treats you that way. The bot-tom line is this: "I am not available to be spoken to that way, and if you want to have a relationship with me, you must be willing to agree not to engage in that behavior any longer."

A boundary might support and protect your capacity. For exam-ple, "My plate is full at the moment, and I'm unable to take on any more projects," or "No," or "Thanks for thinking of me, but I am not available that day." A boundary might be an understanding that you have with yourself about what is within your realm of responsibility and what is not. You might, for example, set a boundary with yourself that doesn't allow you to jump your fence to muck around in someone else's realm of responsibility by helping in ways that have not been requested or by taking responsibility in another way for something that is theirs to own.

Building on your realm of responsibility, the following practice urges you to take stock of the boundaries that exist in your life and illuminate the places in your life where these boundaries might not exist or are routinely trampled upon. Getting into alignment with your values sets the groundwork for setting boundaries because it shows you what your physical, emotional, mental, and spiritual priorities are. If your boundaries are weak or unclear, you are more prone to take responsibility for things that don't belong to you and unintentionally give away your personal energy. When you say yes to things that aren't actually in alignment and integrity for you, then of course you don't have the time, energy, or money to devote to what matters most to you. The more you bring your awareness to what is important to you, the more you are able to spend those resources in ways that feel good.

Journal prompts to dive deeper:

What messages have you been taught over the course of your life about setting boundaries?

What boundaries do you have in place in your life now?

What boundaries do you wish you could set, even if you don't yet know how?

What do you find yourself feeling routinely angry or resentful about? What would you do in that situation if you could do or ask for anything?

What support do you imagine you will need as you begin experimenting with setting boundaries?

A way to begin experimenting with establishing boundaries and coming into greater alignment is to notice what you're doing right now and to get curious about why you are doing it. Generally speaking, our allegiance is almost always to ourselves, even when we may not realize it. Everything we do is in service of meeting a need—often for safety or belonging. And there's nothing wrong with that. If you aren't clear what needs are motivating you, you'll likely take actions that don't actually take care of the need, get caught up in boundary violations, or have you taking responsibility for something that is not yours to be responsible for. Remember, you are responsible for your needs, and your job is to stay out of other people's realm of responsibilities. You've been doing everything you've been doing in your life for a good reason. And there's still some need not being met. (After all, you're reading this book.) The more you do this work, bringing yourself back to your own inner landscape and no longer externalizing your safety and belonging, the better you'll get to know your needs and the better you'll be able to honor them. When you're conscious of your primary allegiance to yourself and are acting on it intentionally, you will operate from a place of truly knowing what you are available for when somebody asks you for a favor or whenever you are in a situation where you're trying to figure out how to get your needs met in relationship with other people.

Practice: The Hot-Potato Collector

Navigating relationships and interactions with others while remaining in integrity with yourself can be a lot like playing the children's game Hot Potato. (Even navigating your relationship with YOURSELF can become a game of Hot Potato.) Something I noticed about myself when I started to get a handle on my integrity and prioritized my needs was that I was basically just carrying around a gigantic basket of hot potatoes. It was as if people were throwing hot potatoes at me all day long, and I was gladly receiving them because I have always felt comfortable taking care of other people's emotions and discomfort and taking responsibility for making things easier. Because I was disconnected from my integrity, the question of whether I actually *wanted* the hot potato didn't even come up for me.

Many of us don't know what to do with our uncomfortable feelings or responsibilities, and passing them off to someone else is a very convenient way to get rid of them, making our problem *their* problem (or hot potato) so that we don't have to deal with it any longer. Humans who carry marginalized identities, women, and those of us who were assigned female at birth are often socialized to alchemize discomfort, making us excellent hot-potato gatherers, regardless of the hot potato's impact on our health and well-being.

Your job is to stop picking up every hot potato that's thrown your way. I like to envision myself wearing a full-body rain suit that the hot potato slides right off of. I find this way of thinking about it really useful because when we think about it as a physical object, we can start to visualize what is happening with our energy.

You don't want to deal with this thing. It's hot. You want to get rid of it. You're tossing it over to me, and I'm picking it up.

Picking up this hot potato isn't your job, whether you're doing so because you're trying to fix something for someone or taking responsibility for the discomfort because you're accustomed to dealing with it. More often than not, that hot potato is outside of your fence and realm of responsibility. The more clear you can be about your boundaries and remain in integrity with yourself, the more clear you can be about what you are energetically picking up as you move about in the world, and the more energy you will have in your own life.

START HERE

Bring your focus to the infinitesimal space between you and the rest of the world around you. Imagine this space as a thin ring of light around your body. Like the fence around your inner landscape, inside this ring of light is your sacred, sovereign terrain. This is where your thoughts, feelings, actions, reactions, and the consequences of your actions live. This is your land to tend. This expansive, wild vista encompasses everything that is yours to own, take responsibility for, and nurture. I bring your attention to this ring of light because this practice seeks to teach you how to thicken this subtle border.

On the other side of the ring of light is everything that belongs to everyone else around you. *Their beliefs. Their actions. Their mistakes. The consequences of their worst moments. Their needs. Their dreams for their lives. Their feelings. Their reactions. Their personal process for getting it done, which might be enraging, terrifying, or confusing to witness. That is their terrain.*

Many of us are suffering from a lack of tending because our boundaries are too porous or lack structural integrity. We are all carrying the pain of not being permitted or encouraged to relish our sovereignty, believe our needs matter, or expect our humanity to be respected by all the other humans in our lives.

You are allowed to be the sentient, imperfect, feeling, emotional, curious, hilarious, flawed, healed, and healing human that you are. Your job is to bring your attention to your subtle border and start to notice when you trespass your own boundaries, whether you take in someone else's judgment, carry someone else's belief about how something should get done, or extend yourself before someone has asked for your help. You do not have to accept every hot potato offered to you. You are allowed to remain in integrity with yourself and your wants, even when that integrity says, "I do not want this potato."

Ask yourself, *What hot potato am I unwilling to pick up today?*

This work is not instantaneous. It is the consistent practice of noticing that what someone has offered you is OPTIONAL for you to pick up and making a choice about how to proceed that honors you and your needs.

Make the best choice that you can about how to proceed with the tools you have on hand.

Forgive yourself for being a work in progress, because as you practice this skill, you will make mistakes and find your way back to familiar patterns of minimizing your needs or overdelivering. Practice this skill anyway.

THIS MIGHT LOOK LIKE . . .

If you're at the self-responsibility stage, this might look like reminding yourself as many times as you need to that someone else's bad mood, need, or stress is not a letterpress invitation to involve yourself in their process or rescue them from their discomfort.

If you're at the self-care stage, this might look like beginning to notice where you too are tossing unwanted emotions at the people in your life when you feel uncomfortable, attempting to offload your discomfort or make it their problem.

If you're at the self-trust stage, this might look like realizing that your tendency to overinvolve yourself in others' lives has deep roots. How has this pattern of behavior served you? What does distracting yourself in this way save you from? How might you care for those needs instead of distracting from them?

If you're at the self-love stage, this might look like turning your awareness toward those moments when a hot potato is flung your way or when you want to discard your undesired emotions. Get curious about those moments. What needs are revealing themselves? How can you care for those needs?

If you're at the advocacy stage, this might look like having a conversation with the hot-potato thrower and outlining what you are and aren't willing to take responsibility for, particularly if it is someone you are in close relationship with. When Sharon's partner was getting sober, her partner began to have angry outbursts. Sharon, a self-described people pleaser, struggled during these outbursts, believing the story that her partner's "negative" emotions were a sign Sharon had done something wrong or should work harder. Sharon was working hard in an attempt to protect herself from her partner's anger instead of addressing it directly, but this was only making her resentful. One day Sharon was able to tell her partner that when she yelled, it made her feel like she was getting in trouble even though she didn't think she had done anything wrong. Sharon was able to set a boundary. She loved her partner and respected that many feelings were coming up for her during her process of getting sober. And she was aware she didn't have the capacity to process her partner's anger with her. Sharon's partner understood her concerns and went out and got a therapist the next day.

Tending to Your Capacity to Care

We are in an overwhelming and fully engulfing moment in history where we are collectively and individually grappling with the ever-present effects of the climate emergency; uncertainty in the face of waves and the aftermath of the global COVID-19 pandemic; and policies that impact the daily lives, safety, and voting rights of communities that have been historically and systemically marginalized. Many are reeling as we attempt to grapple with the constant media onslaught, level of civic engagement, and meager attempts to tend to ourselves (if we remember to tend at all). It can be challenging to balance efforts to participate in social justice movements and cocreate cultures of change without navigating compassion fatigue. Many of us are rethinking what we stand for and how we embody those commitments without continually falling prey to the roller coaster of burnout.

In an attempt to create positive change, you might find yourself in a familiar pattern of overcommitting yourself, overextending the limits of your human capacity, and placing the urgency of the causes you are devoted to above your own needs.

So, how do you care for yourself and remain in integrity in a world overflowing with urgent collective needs? The truth is you need yourself and your boundaries now more than ever. Your needs are not *less* important in the face of human suffering but *more* important. We need one another now more than ever. Devoting yourself to your tending isn't frivolous or selfish but necessary if you are going to sustain your commitments to the world around you.

What are you committed to, right now? How are you ready, able, and willing to devote your precious resources—your time, energy, attention, and cash—to those commitments? What is in integrity for you? You cannot be committed to everything. Similar to the practice of prioritizing in this chapter, your efforts will be far more effective if you can focus on the specific commitments you are genuinely able to make. These commitments may change over the course of your life, but having them enables you to create a greater intended impact instead of paying lip service to your values or partially engaging in a distracted and overwhelmed way. What do you have to offer to the world around you? How can you make an impact in a way that feels true to you, harnessing the skills you have to share and aligning with your values? You might feel uncomfortable choosing only one or two causes to focus your attention on, but in doing so, you are able to deepen your impact and hone your approach.

Ask yourself: *What am I committed to right now? What really matters to me? What is in integrity for me?*

As you define these commitments for yourself, get curious about what you personally require to make good on them. What nourishes you? What do you need to thoughtfully engage from a deeply grounded place? What sustains your energy so that you can bring your most robust self to the work throughout your life? How can you pace yourself to ensure you won't burn out or give up? How can you temper your feelings of urgency to make your work more sustainable? It is easy to fall into the belief that slowing down or creating a more sustainable system of support will negatively impact your efforts, but how can you be of service to anyone if you forget to serve yourself?

Traditional self-care can be pigeonholed as self-obsessed navel-gazing, but tending to your capacity to care and approaching your life from a place of alignment and integrity are anything but. What actions are in integrity for you, and how are you willing to support yourself to ensure that you have the capacity to make good on those actions? This is how you ensure you are in the position to care in a way that is flexible and steadfast. What may once have been considered a selfish disregard for others is transformed into collective change when we sustainably pour our energy into the corners of our community and world.

Commitments to My Need for Integrity

— My body, life, and energy are mine to enjoy and use as I see fit. Living this—acting in accordance with my values—is how I develop integrity.

— Integrity is a need most of us are conditioned to ignore. We are taught to act in accordance with our conditioning or with the wants of those around us. This disconnection from self leads to exhausting dissonance. This disconnection is not my fault, but reconnection is my responsibility. I begin by getting a good sense of what my values actually are.

— One really common way to get out of alignment is to become a hot-potato collector. I am only responsible for myself, my needs, and my wants (and maybe those of a child). I do not have to pick up the potatoes.

— Building this kind of integrity with myself increases my capacity to care in ways that are absolutely crucial for building trust in my relationship with myself and expanding my capacity to care for myself.

CHAPTER 7

Sovereignty

BLESSING

I am a powerful creator. I lead my life with compassion, gentle discipline, and undisputed sovereignty. I invest my precious resources in maintaining my capacity, my sacred vessel for impacting change in my own life and the lives of those around me. I prioritize anything and everything I require, including drenching myself in life-generating pleasure, play, and the distinct joy of fully embodying a life tailor-fit for me.

I am a devoted, tender steward of my physical, mental, emotional, and spiritual bodies. I am benevolent in my leadership, committed to tending the landscape I was given, caring for THIS body and life, instead of spending my precious resources wishing myself away in the face of my perceived flaws. No longer interested in fragmenting, folding, or fracturing the aspects of my being for external approval, I am committed to bringing my whole self with me wherever I go.

I give myself permission to begin again as many times as I need. I do not need to wait for the fresh start of a new day, week, month, or year. I can choose to grant myself a fresh start whenever I need it.

I am responsible for the quality of my inner life. I am responsible for the experience of being on the receiving end of my self-talk. I am responsible for disentangling myself from systems, beliefs, and relationships that do not accept or appreciate me in my fullness.

Being responsible for and taking care of myself aren't optional. I matter, deeply. There is no one in my life more deserving of my consistency, courage, strength, ingenuity, compassion, and intelligence than I am.

I am pulling myself into the epicenter of my life and reasserting my mattering through my daily actions. I will no longer wait until it feels better, easier, or less complicated to care for myself.

> I will no longer wait until I have the right outfit, body, words,
> planner, or depth of understanding. I am committed to taking
> one imperfect action and then another.

FIVE YEARS AGO I was visiting the dentist for tooth pain. I told him I had been avoiding chewing on one side of my mouth because I was afraid there was a crack in one of my teeth. The dentist, unalarmed by my alarm that SOMETHING HORRIBLE was happening in my mouth, said simply, "Look, just chew on it like normal. Then at least we'll know if there is an issue. Avoiding the tooth isn't a sustainable strategy. If a problem presents itself, we will fix it."

What struck me in the days that followed my visit was that I had been using that same unsustainable strategy in some of my relationships. This "strategy" was pretending to be something I wasn't, saying yes to things I wanted to say no to, and bending myself into different shapes to meet my need for belonging. The "big scary thing" was being rejected for who I truly was and what I wanted.

How long had I been pretending? How long had I
believed I needed to micromanage other people's
perceptions of me—working to always, always
present myself in the best possible light?

The dentist was right. Chewing on one side of my mouth so that I never had to face the possibility of a chipped tooth head-on wasn't a sustainable way to live—and neither was believing I needed to show up in a certain way to win external approval in my relationships. The fear that kept me chewing on one side of my mouth for a year also taught me to deny my needs and desires, until I woke up one day in a life I didn't know and didn't like, panicked because I might never find my way out.

A few years later, the big scary thing happened.

A person who knew me very well and I believed loved me got angry and used it as an opportunity to tell me all the things about myself they had never liked. The tooth cracked. It was more painful than I imagined it would be. Although there was an inciting incident, I've come to realize the rift between us began years before—whenever I expressed confidence or unchecked enthusiasm about my work or my life. As my confidence grew, so did the rift, until our communication was thick and tense. For a time, I did what I had always done: I acquiesced, smushing myself into the tiniest box I could because I was afraid of the conflict that might erupt at any moment. Even after all of the work I had done with myself, I was still terrified of conflict, unsure whether I could trust myself to have my own back when everything in me wanted to run, hide, and please my way out.

The painful truth was that in all of my pleasing, I had been dishonest with both of us. My silence cosigned my friend's behavior and rubberstamped my discomfort in the face of it. It took years to realize the relationship might have been saved if I had felt strong enough to speak up for myself and share my truth. It was a lesson that emotional intimacy is necessary to cocreate a relationship that works for both or all parties. I couldn't expect anyone to read my mind, and I couldn't twist myself into more kind, loving, and compassionate shapes hoping someone might get the hint and reciprocate in kind.

The moment the relationship broke wasn't dramatic. My friend was mad about an error they believed I made and used the opportunity to tell me all the things they had stored up about me that they took issue with. As I was listening to their description of me, I felt a deep and unyielding NO forming in my body. While I will fess up to being a person of many faults, I flatly disagreed with their depiction of me and my motives. For the first time in my life, I was not willing to shrink to accommodate or take it on, so I didn't. My ego wanted to shout back and correct the record, but when it came down to it, I didn't have much energy for that either. I simply walked away.

In the end, my heart was broken. I loved someone who deeply hurt my feelings. I trusted them, even after years and years of not trusting friendships or another's ability to hold and uplift me in my fullness.

The hole that their presence left in my life is one I have fallen into daily since that last conversation, but I am grateful for it too. I was grateful to feel that no. I was grateful to identify a boundary for how I was willing to be treated in a relationship for the first time. I was grateful to have had my own back. I was grateful to have prized my sovereignty, even when it led to painful experiences.

On the other side of this friend breakup and a few others, I was surprised to realize the relationships that remain are ones where I feel deeply loved, appreciated, and welcome to show up exactly as I am. These are relationships where conflict is safe, needs are expressed and attended to, boundaries are celebrated, and sovereignty is central.

I share this story because I know the deep fear of worrying you will be rejected or abandoned if you start asking for what you need and stepping into your full power.

Here's the truth: You might. And that might really be okay.

At that moment, I made a new choice for the first time in my life— the choice to remain sovereign, by my own side, loving and approving of myself, instead of immediately shrinking myself into whatever version of me they wanted instead.

I spent the following years imagining and reimagining our final conversation, each time coming back to an essential question. Is it safe to be myself and take up space even if it costs me a relationship?

But here's the thing: the tooth was already an issue. I was avoiding dealing with that by pretending I could chew on one side of my mouth forever. The relationship was already broken. Haunted by the painful loss of attachment during my formative years, I had been avoiding dealing with more loss by pretending I was a much less sparkly, full-bodied, opinionated version of myself. I was lying to myself by believing it was my job to diminish myself in order to hold the relationship together. I was lying to myself by believing this was the kind of friendship I wanted and that I should feel lucky someone wanted to have me around. I was lying to myself by believing I was too small or too scared to deal with the ramifications of the unknown, of what would happen if I started showing up as I am.

I share this story because sometimes we skirt the potential ramifications of how our lives and relationships will shift when we step into our sovereignty and self-belonging. We skirt because the potential pain seems too scary. Because we have settled "comfortably" into our relationship contracts, believing we need to be a certain way to keep the relationship or to be loved at all. Because if we knew the cost of showing up for ourselves and prioritizing our needs, maybe we would never begin.

But no matter what your fear is, any problems that are going to happen are going to happen. Just chew on it like normal. Show up as your whole self however and whenever possible. If a problem presents itself, you will fix it.

You Are the Leader of Your Life

Sovereignty is self-responsibility in action. It is the daily decision to lead from the center of your life, making your decisions alongside a nuanced understanding of your own finite energetic capacity, personal and collective values, and deeply felt truth. At its best, sovereignty is the choice to become a benevolent leader, generous in your tending and hell-bent on allowing and honoring the entirety of your lived experience, if only within the lush wilderness of your inner landscape. Sovereignty isn't the opposite of dependence or commitment to others. It is always in service to the health and well-being of our relationships. It is the boundary around our realm of responsibility, our deep understanding of what is our work and what isn't. Approaching your life from a rooted place of sovereignty enables you to co-create relationships that are truthful for both parties and in which you both feel safe to bring your full self.

However, at the beginning, sovereignty can be as small as taking an interest in your own experience. You have a deep need for a life guided by what feels best and right to YOU, specifically, which is why a life determined by external markers of success and validation never truly satisfies. Becoming the sovereign leader of your life means turning toward yourself first when making your decisions instead of looking first to the world for a universally approved path forward. Reclaiming your sovereignty requires you to actively participate in your daily choices as you learn to rebuild your life with self-leadership and self-tending. Not perfectly. Oftentimes, messily. And still, sovereign.

As the sovereign leader of your life, granting yourself permission to be who you are, love what you love, and approach everything in your life in a way that works for you are your ultimate responsibilities. Tending to these responsibilities requires investigating the belief systems you carry around what it means to do enough and be enough. It begs you to look deep into the ways you might be outsourcing your power and waiting for someone to read your mind to know what you want and need. It urges you to dismantle your perfectionism and increase your tolerance for allowing your true human self to exist. Stepping into your sovereignty means no longer waiting for someone else to tell you you've done enough or that it's time to turn your energy back toward yourself. It means you are the final word on how you define yourself, even as your identities shift beneath your touch.

Waiting for someone else to give you permission to be who and how you are gives the other people in your life the job of determining your worthiness. The people you have been hoping will notice and validate you are caught up in their own sets of needs and reckoning with their own enoughness. Relying on another's permission and validation not only trespasses against your sovereignty, it also overlooks the other person's experience, who likely does not realize you're relying on them to handle your most precious sense of worthiness when they interact with you.

By determining for yourself what is enough, you learn to tend to your vision for your life with love, compassion, and gentle discipline. It takes discipline to remind yourself to be kind and generous when you speak to yourself. It takes discipline to take your daily decisions off autopilot and remain conscious. It takes discipline to stay connected to your vision for your life, especially when doing so challenges ingrained systems or the established relationship contracts you have with the humans in your life.

The more data you collect and the more attention you pay to yourself, the more comfortable and confident you will feel making decisions on your own behalf. This confidence is built through promises made and kept, and data mined from experiences and put to good use. You are always in the process of a relationship with yourself and always in the process of refining that relationship—doing it just a little bit differently than you may have done it last time.

By defying your perfectionism and giving yourself permission to take action in your own right timing, you learn what it means to hold yourself lovingly accountable, without judgment or cruelty. You do not need to love yourself unconditionally to respect yourself, and taking responsibility for your life is more about respect than love. It is your job to tend to the glorious life you were given, instead of spending your life comparing yourself to others, particularly when you are comparing yourself to the ideal version of you that lives in your imagination. Your ideal self is the perfect marriage of you at your very best and the social conditioning you've absorbed throughout your life. Your ideal self is familiar enough to keep you hooked into striving for that level of perfection, but it is by design both a figment of your imagination and permanently out of reach. Your ideal self is not you but a weapon you use to punish yourself and keep yourself in line. No matter how much you might wish for it, your ideal self is not coming to save you from your awkward, messy humanity, even if you work as hard as possible to achieve that level of perfection.

Remember, each experience is an opportunity to either build or destroy self-trust. Your sovereignty doesn't end with shifts in your daily choices. It also encompasses taking responsibility for how you speak to yourself about those choices and their outcomes. Pay attention to the expectations you have of yourself each day. Are they reasonable—meaning, are they expectations that your true human self can reasonably meet? Are they malleable, responsive to your feelings and needs over the course of your daily life? Do you check in with yourself, making adjustments to your expectations as you monitor your energetic capacity throughout your week? Or are they mandates based on what you believe your ideal self should be able to accomplish? Again, your ideal self is a figment of your imagination. Basing your expectations on what your ideal self should be able to accomplish is not only a disservice but also abusive. You are the only one in your body, and thus the only one who knows what you have the energy for on any given day. This conversation becomes infinitely more reliable as you work to be in relationship with yourself and prioritize your connection with yourself.

You have the opportunity to reclaim your sovereignty each time you turn to yourself to determine what feels right instead of immediately looking outside yourself for answers. There is incredible freedom in this reclamation. Imagine what it might be like to no longer wait for someone else's validation! Imagine how empowered you will feel making decisions on your own behalf once you teach yourself there is no "right" or "wrong" answer, just YOUR answer!

Journal prompts to dive deeper:

What permission have you been waiting for?

What might be different for you if you believed you had the permission you ache for?

What thoughts or feelings come up for you when you consider stepping into your power as your own permission granter?

What fears do you notice arise when you think about reclaiming your sovereignty and no longer outsourcing your enoughness? What do you imagine might happen?

In clear language, what are the words you need to hear from yourself at this moment?

Daily Acts of Sovereignty

Each moment over the course of your day is an opportunity to turn toward yourself to make decisions that are in alignment with who you are and what you really want. These decisions include microdecisions, such as what you want to eat for breakfast, what you want to wear today, and what items to put in your grocery cart, as well as bigger decisions about next career or relationship steps. Each and every choice is a chance to turn toward yourself, get curious, and ask: "Well, what would I like to do? What would I do if nobody ever told me what to do? What would I do naturally if I didn't have an overdeveloped ability to know exactly what is expected of me?"

Reclaiming these daily choices can be both a subtle reorganization of your priorities and a massive shift in how you approach your life. Too often we fall into routines and habits based on who we have been, what we were taught was good, or who we think we should be to earn external approval, instead of grounding our routines in who we are at this moment and what we need in the present. Your identity is not fixed. You are not who you were yesterday. Being a sovereign leader requires that you care enough about the felt-experience of your life to patiently check in with yourself frequently and make sure your choices are still in alignment. When you work to create a life spacious and uniquely shaped to fit your multitudes, you show yourself that you matter. Being in daily relationship with yourself is the ultimate self-care practice.

As always, giving yourself permission to be who and how you are is a muscle you develop through practice. As you work through the prompts in this chapter, remember that granting yourself permission may feel clunky, but that doesn't mean you are doing it wrong. Furthermore, showing up in the world as you are is tricky when you have a history of people-pleasing or overachieving. Making decisions for yourself that are rooted in what feels right for you means giving up an essential coping mechanism—looking outside yourself to determine your safety. This can feel incredibly vulnerable, *and* it is essential for developing a trustworthy relationship with yourself. Feelings of vulnerability don't mean you're doing this wrong. They mean you're human. Be kind to yourself as you invite more and more of yourself into the center of your life.

Journal prompts to dive deeper:

What is currently working in your life?

What is not currently working in your life?

How might you express yourself in your relationships if you felt safe and welcomed to do so?

How might you dress or adorn yourself if you felt safe and welcomed to do so?

What might you do differently if you felt safe and welcomed to do so?

What do you love that you secretly judge yourself for?

Practice: Being the Detective of Your Own Experience

To stand in your power and sovereignty, you must commit to paying attention to yourself with open eyes and an open heart as you collect data about your experiences. Every moment. Every phone call. Every time you get dressed. Every time your heart is broken. Every time you disappoint yourself. Every time you are triggered and you react instantaneously. It is all data, data that is essential if you are to make more aligned decisions moving forward.

This practice invites you to become a detective of your experiences and to communicate with yourself honestly in an effort to create more aligned, sovereign, and authentic experiences in the future. For example, let's say you went to a party at a coworker's home. You got dressed up and spent the night dancing with your friends. You had a good time, despite the fact that you were allergic to most of the food that was served and that one of your coworkers hit on you repeatedly despite your requests he redirect his attention elsewhere. Each experience holds powerful data about each of us. You now know you love the bright lipstick you were wearing, the music played at the party, and the festive feeling of being out late at night. You also know that next time you need to set better boundaries with your coworker and bring something delicious and more in tune with your body's needs to add to the menu. The more data that you accumulate about yourself, the better equipped you will be to make sovereign decisions on your own behalf, and the only way to gather this data is to put yourself out there and have experiences.

While the daily details might vary in their level of importance to you, the process of paying attention to and caring about your personal experience is powerfully validating. This practice is an act of choosing to matter to yourself enough to take the time to sit with your experiences instead of muscling through them or pushing your feelings out of the way. The data you acquire here can be the difference between a future experience that feels custom-created for you and one where you feel overlooked and unimportant, yet again.

Once you begin tracking the moments that light you up, you can begin incorporating them into your life intentionally. You could wear that pink lipstick to the grocery store or listen to a playlist of your favorite songs while you wash the dishes or suggest a late-night spot for your next gathering with your friends. You can take this data and use it to incorporate more joy and truth into your life as you continue making better and more aligned decisions on your own behalf. Becoming a detective of your own experience is the step-by-step process of getting to know and learning to like yourself. This can actually be a pleasurable process, as long as you can muster up a giggle when you find yourself at a meetup group for forty-something lovers of Wes Anderson movies and realize it's totally not your scene. This process requires some trial and error.

START HERE

What activities have brought you joy in your life? Write them down. These can be activities you liked as far in the past as when you were 5, 14, during your "punk phase," when you were in college, as well as during your last relationship.

There may not be many of them. That's okay.

Now think about activities you've seen other people doing that have stopped you in your tracks and made you wonder if you might like doing that too. Write those things down.

This is a running list, so please add to it as you move through your life. I guarantee you that half of the activities on your list won't live up to your expectations. But some of them will. The point here is to actively participate in your life, muck around a bit, test the waters, and try something ridiculous in the name of creating a life that feels like a perfect fit for you. If you can stay open and present, you will be rewarded with the confidence of knowing each moment is ripe for learning how to better care for yourself.

Develop a system for determining how you felt about something you've done. Ask yourself:

How did this make me feel?

Would I do it again?

Did it fill me up or deplete me?

Did I feel pressured to like it? Did I like it because I thought it would increase my safety?

What were the parts I liked best?

Repeat this activity as you examine the many parts of the day you may have put on autopilot—the choices you make without consciously realizing you are making a choice. Take those decisions off autopilot and examine them. Ask yourself: *Is this really what I want to do? Is there a way that this could feel more sustainable and pleasurable?* As you experiment, you will learn so much about what you enjoy and what you don't. Ultimately, creating an intentional and joyful life is making the conscious choice to do more of what makes you feel good and less of what doesn't.

THIS MIGHT LOOK LIKE . . .

If you're at the self-responsibility stage, this might look like taking your daily choices off autopilot and beginning small experiments to fill daily moments with delight, like pouring yourself a cup of coffee in your favorite mug or deciding what toothpaste to buy.

If you're at the self-care stage, this might look like weaving joy and celebration into everything you do by asking yourself what might make even the most mundane commitment an ounce more pleasurable.

If you're at the self-trust stage, this might look like looking around your living space or through your closet and asking what reflects you and supports you in feeling like the fullest, most vibrant version of yourself. Is there something you could add or alter to make your surroundings or wardrobe feel MORE like you? Do it.

If you're at the self-love stage, this might look like dressing how YOU want to dress, eating food YOU find delicious and beautiful, decorating your living space in a way that brings YOU joy. There is no end to the ways to delight yourself each day, and you are thrilled about finding new ways to express yourself.

If you're at the advocacy stage, this might look like sharing your preferences with the humans in your life. Invite them into your bespoke moments. Ask for the specific flavor of what you're hungering for. Give them feedback about how you might want to do things differently next time.

Practice: Saying No. Saying Yes.

All of your newly cultivated truth and trust are leading you to this moment, the moment when you begin to actually make decisions on your own behalf.

You are a sovereign human being and not a robot. In this life, you can do almost anything, but you will not be able to do everything—and you certainly will not be able to do everything all at once. Finding even five minutes in your day to start taking care of yourself likely requires you to say no to something, even when you must say no to yourself. Many of us feel as though our lives are chock-full, and we aren't sure how or why they got that way. We might routinely say yes when we would really like to say no, but we aren't giving ourselves the option to say no, believing that a no will make us less useful, lovable, or worthy. However, each time we say yes when we want to say no, we reinforce the message that we are only worthy when we please others, accommodate their needs ahead of our own, or take responsibility for their discomfort. We are not-so-subtly telling ourselves that we matter less than the people around us, that our sovereignty is up for grabs.

WHEN TO SAY NO

When the mere mention of the thing fills you with anger or resentment.

When you've lost your love or energy for a project.

When you're only saying yes because you want someone to like you.

When you really wish you could say no but can't find the words.

When there is something else you'd really rather do.

When you're only saying yes because you feel like you should.

When you're continuing to say yes because you are scared of what other people will think (or say) about you if you change your mind.

HOW TO SAY NO

The outer work of saying no is logistical. Can you give yourself a couple of minutes before definitively responding, so that you don't have to do it on the spot? These few minutes give you time to collect yourself, remember that you've decided to say yes only to things you TRULY want to do, summon your strength, and return to the conversation to say, "No, I'm sorry I'm not going to be able to do that." Write a couple of scripts for yourself for different (and particularly sticky) scenarios. I encourage you to practice them with someone you trust because it helps to be prepared. You may also want to enlist a support team or accountability partner to cheer you on. There is no reason why you have to do it alone.

The inner work of saying no is emotional. Saying no is the practice of believing your time is valuable. It reinforces the message that you are enough as you are and not because of what you do for someone else. This takes time, reminding, and most important, practice. You will gain momentum as you say no more often—and as you start to feel the ease of your day after you've carved out more space for yourself. Write yourself a sticky note. Set an alarm reminder in your phone that it is perfectly okay to say no. Keep a running list of all the times you've said no and the world hasn't come to a crashing halt. Notice the moments when other people successfully say no, and notice how you probably still love them anyway.

The next time someone asks you to do something you truly don't want to do, say no.

There is no kiddie pool for this one. It's going to take some guts. But it is not your job to say yes to everyone and lose yourself in the mix. It is not your job to take responsibility for all of the things all of the time. You are allowed to rest and play. But to say yes to yourself, you have to teach yourself how to say no.

If you are not yet ready to say no to a real live human, experiment with a few quiet ways of saying no:

— Unfollow or mute someone you no longer wish to follow on social media.

— Stop reading a book if you are truly not enjoying it.

— Put down your phone and close your eyes when you crave rest but are stuck scrolling.

— Ask yourself what you REALLY want to listen to while you drive to work in the morning.

ON SAYING YES

What will you do with all of your newly found, reclaimed time, space, and energy? Say yes to yourself! It is important to remember that saying no and saying yes work together here. One carves out the space, and the other cultivates microexperiences of pleasure throughout your day. This pleasure might be joyful, restful, or rejuvenating. It might be the distinct enjoyment of working on the things you want and need to take care of instead of something you put in your life to please someone else. There is unbelievable power in choosing to align more deeply with your natural instinct. Each time you say yes to yourself, you reinforce the belief that your pleasure matters and is worthy to be prioritized in the scheme of your life.

As you experiment with your yeses here, remember how we redefined readiness at the beginning of the book. A yes doesn't necessarily mean a full-throttle, full-bodied HELL YES. It doesn't require the absence of fear or reservation. You might find a yes tucked into a moment of curiosity or resonance. You might find your body softening as it responds to an idea or an invitation. You might find your yes bound up in a moment of thorny jealousy about something someone else has acquired, made happen, or created. These more subtle moments are yeses too, even if you have routinely diminished or overlooked them. By saying no, you carve out more space to be in relationship with yourself, attuning yourself to the more subtle desires that have been dancing just outside your attention. The more you coax these preferences and dreams forward, the more willingly they will present themselves in the future. The more space you are ready, able, and willing to create for yourself, the more space you'll have for prioritizing your yeses.

THIS MIGHT LOOK LIKE . . .

If you're at the self-responsibility stage, this might look like acknowledging and honoring the times when you have said yes though you really wanted to say no, even if you didn't realize it until after the fact.

If you're at the self-care stage, this might look like giving yourself space to respond when someone asks you for something. You might still feel as though you need to say yes when you want to say no, but having the space to consider it on your own terms is important work in and of itself.

If you're at the self-trust stage, this might look like knowing you can say no, even if it makes someone else angry or upset when you do. You are responsible for and to yourself. They are allowed to react however they react, and then you get to choose how to respond next.

If you're at the self-love stage, this might look like understanding that when you say no, your yeses will be energetically clear. This means the people in your life can rest easy and receive from you. What a beautiful feeling!

If you're at the advocacy stage, this might look like saying no when you want to say no. Even when it feels scary. Even when your voice shakes. If this feels too intense to attempt, try beginning with someone who feels safe. Giving yourself permission to build this muscle with use doesn't mean you have to automatically go for the most intimidating no. You can work up to it. Practice saying no when the stakes are low. Ellen felt an intense surge of fear whenever she wanted to say no. She felt guilty about letting the person in front of her down and feared they would think less of her. With time and experience saying a lot of yeses she wished she could take back as soon as they left her mouth, Ellen told her closest friend this was something she was practicing and asked if her friend would be willing to be patient with her while she worked on it in their relationship. Ellen knew the process of getting more comfortable saying no would mean she would initially say yes and then have to go back and change her mind. Having this plan in place with a close friend helped her figure out when and how she wanted to say no, while knowing her friend was there to support her in doing so. It was often uncomfortable, but it got much easier with practice. With time, Ellen was able to expand the circle of people she felt comfortable saying no to, especially as she realized how much energy it freed up for her. She had to focus on allowing other people to have their feelings about her nos, and she had to remind herself again and again that she was not responsible for managing their discomfort. This process took a bit of time and perseverance, but Ellen felt incredible confidence and freedom on the other side of it.

Hands in the Dirt: Permission to Show Up Messy

"I guess the thing is I don't want it to be me. I don't want to be the one responsible for my needs. I am so exhausted from being responsible for myself for so long," my client said after a long pause.

On the other end of the line, I said flatly, "The honest truth is that I don't want it to be me either, even though I know in my bones it is."

How human of us.

Suddenly I was in college again, sitting on the floor in my closet with a fistful of bills from student accounts. Ordinarily so responsible, I couldn't bring myself to open the bills and make the call to set up the loans to cover them. I felt bone-tired and simultaneously ridiculous. I was 20 years old and weary from a lifetime of holding myself to an impossible, unreachable standard of responsibility in order to feel remotely safe.

I could feel my client's exhaustion through the phone. "I've been doing it all for so long. I guess I just wanted someone else to take care of me for once. I thought if I made myself better or got married or was more lovable, someone would take care of me. I didn't expect to have to do it all myself."

This is where the wound is: *If I were more worthy, someone would scoop me up and care for me. If I were more lovable, someone would save me from my life by reading my mind and anticipating all my needs. If I deserved to have my needs met, they would have been met when I was a child. If I work harder, I might earn my way to the care and rest I require.*

This is the wound that keeps us out of our power and sovereignty, when we bend ourselves into shapes to metabolize the discomfort present in the room around us, exhausted from trying to be everything to everyone to earn our peace, lying when we say yes but really want to say no, not speaking our truth because we are deeply afraid it might come at the cost of our belonging. This wound tells us that the fix for what ails us is *somewhere out there*, in someone else's hands, and we will earn it **if only** we work hard enough, instead of meeting ourselves smack dab in the middle of our discomfort and remaining by our own side.

Yes, you might be exhausted from a lifetime of overresponsibility. Yes, you deserved to be held and cared for. Yes, it might make perfect sense that you are too tired from all that labor and don't want to take care of yourself, attempting instead to outsource your care to the people around you. How human of you. And you are the sovereign leader of your life. There is no one coming to save you from yourself.

This is your moment to coax yourself back into the center of your life and begin operating out of that place of personal power. Even when it breaks your heart. Even when your voice shakes. Even when you change your mind a million times before you get it right. To be in right relationship with yourself means you operate from the middle of your life, with care and kindness for your capacity and sustainable action. That is your job. Doing that job in large and small ways each day is how you meet your need for sovereignty.

I carefully reminded my client she might be less exhausted if she handed back some of what she was holding together. "This is an invitation to do less. Let your first act of care be tending to your lifetime of exhaustion. This isn't about racing off somewhere. It is about taking care of what is, and what is for you right now is a need for rest. Stop trying to have it all together to project an image of who you think other people want and need you to be. Be messy. Give yourself permission to show up messy."

When I say show up messy, what I really mean is: show up. Show up as you are. Keep showing up. Let your humanity seep through. Disappoint people in your effort to stop disappointing yourself. Get it wrong. Do it again. Let people connect with you, the real you, not the you camouflaged beneath layers of forced attempts at perfection.

Moments like these—big or small—are opportunities to rebuild your self-trust. They are the exact perfect moment to turn your attention to the words you are using to describe yourself in your own mind and to determine whether these words affirm and generate trust. They are your chance to stand in your sovereignty as a human who can take responsibility for the quality and trajectory of your life, without needing to do so perfectly for it to matter or count. This rebuilding is relational. It requires conversation and experimentation. You heal aspects of past losses of self-trust by turning toward yourself with genuine curiosity about what happened last time and how you might make an effort to show up for yourself even just the tiniest bit more this time.

Your body is a trustworthy teacher. Your feelings are signposts, guiding you back to your needs. Your needs illuminate your basic requirements for thriving in all of your relationships, including the one with yourself. You build trust as you turn toward yourself and prioritize the felt-experience of your life. You build trust when you take the time and dig deep for the patience required to ask yourself what is true for you and then hold space for that truth in whatever way feels right.

These tools enable you to make decisions on your own behalf, teaching you how to show up sovereign for what you care about most in a way that is sustainable and kind. These are the mechanics of taking action in your life while staying by your own side. This is how you build the trust to know you will show up to do what needs to be done without being unnecessarily cruel to yourself. These aren't skills you can read about and somehow magically know how to use them perfectly. Instead, I am inviting you to climb into the muck of it with yourself. Dig your hands in the dirt. Ask yourself how it feels. Return to your breath, your feelings, and the needs of your physical body over and over again to fine-tune your approach.

Commitments to My Need for Sovereignty

— I have a need for autonomy, the ability to live a life guided by what I value and deem essential. No one else can fulfill this need for me. And I will never meet it perfectly.

— Reclaiming my sovereignty is an act of permission and responsibility. I am solely responsible for deciding what enoughness looks like. I tend to my own needs. I give myself permission.

— Sovereignty is not permissiveness. Sovereignty is not, "I'm the only one who determines what matters, so nothing matters and everything's fine, whatever happens, happens!" It is, "I determine what matters, and I take responsibility for meeting my own needs and wants AND remaining in relationship with myself when I fail to do this."

— At its smallest, sovereignty is asking myself in each moment, "What do I want to decide right now?" Each choice is an opportunity to listen to myself and show myself I am going to keep showing up.

— This may be very new to me, and that's completely fine. This is an invitation to become a detective of my own experience and desires. There is no way to do this perfectly. The only thing I can do is try. Messiness is not only okay but encouraged.

— A huge part of this is saying no and saying yes. Until I can truly own my no and my yes, my sovereignty is up for grabs.

CHAPTER 8

Love

BLESSING

This love is not a doing but an undoing.

It is the necessary risk of unlearning everything I've been taught about who and how I should be to connect with who I am and how I feel.

I am not late bills, incomplete work assignments, or hectic afternoons when I overreact and yell. Those are aspects of me, but they do not wholly define me. I am not standing on a stage receiving accolades for the beautiful execution of my life's work. I am not my bitterest moment of darkness, when I fought tooth and nail against the devastating story of my unworthiness.

Each time I was praised for excellence or punished for inadequacy, I learned to see my very humanity as a threat to my belonging. The message was clear: We do not want you as we are. We want you small, perfect, convenient, palatable, and easy to handle.

Unlearning this message is the greatest act of love in my lifetime.

Unconditional, brave self-love means I remain present when I want to abandon myself and care for myself as I would for something or someone I cherish.

Loving myself means reminding myself that my worth is infinite, even when my mind is thick with conditioning that tells me otherwise.

It means claiming my wholeness, the parts of myself I formerly judged and shamed. My wholeness is who I am and is not related to what I do, provide, achieve, earn, or accomplish.

I contain multitudes. My self is composed of my many selves. I make room for each part here, even and especially the parts I feel ashamed of.

I am spectacularly, messily human and also infinitely heroic for choosing to keep showing up.

I matter.

I matter.

I matter.

I WAS ON THE FLOOR IN OUR LIVING ROOM, not quite sure what to say or do next. I had been trying to ask for what I needed, but it required an enormous amount of energy to discern what it was I needed even before I muttered the words aloud. I didn't have any energy left over to tolerate the discomfort of compromising or receiving. It seemed like I asked again and again, but it still wasn't getting me anywhere. I felt ignored. Looked over. Unloved. Because if they really loved me, they would KNOW what I needed. I was trying so hard—to be good, to be clear—and it was useless because no matter what I attempted, I wasn't going to get my needs met.

At that moment, I simply couldn't hold myself together any more as story after old story began tumbling out of the abyss of my body.

I am not deserving of help. I know I am not deserving of help because no one has ever helped me when I needed it.

I am not deserving of help. I know I am not deserving of help because no one ever cared enough about me to notice I desperately needed it without my having to say a word.

I am not deserving of help. But if I never let them know I was broken open and needy, how were they ever supposed to know I needed them?

Am I not deserving of help?

At some point, I had learned to make myself unsinkable. It is a way I learned to safely exist in a world that felt spectacularly unsafe for a little, soft, talkative feeler. It is how I learned to collect responsibilities the way some kids collect stamps or stickers.

The interesting thing about this coping mechanism is how much praise it garnered me over the course of my life. People LOVED that I could be relied upon to hold every minute detail. I could be counted on. With time, I learned to believe my unsinkable self was what people liked best about me, marrying my worth to what I could provide for others.

In reality it is impossible for a human to be truly unsinkable. But there I was, sitting on the living room floor as I felt the things I had tried so hard to lock away somewhere more convenient and out of reach.

I had held it together until I couldn't hold it together anymore. I didn't allow myself to ask for help unless I was experiencing some sort of emergency, and even then, the act of receiving support felt excruciatingly intimate. If I peeled back my carefully shellacked veneer, the people closest to me would see what a mess I was inside. If I asked for help, they might realize they didn't want to associate with someone *like me*.

But what did I really believe I was like underneath it all? What was so bad about me that I didn't deserve the most basic human kindnesses I would wish for anyone? What was so terminally special about me that I didn't need rest, hydration, nourishment, or care?

As I sat there, I wondered aloud who I would be if I no longer told myself the story that I had to be perfect to be loved. If I were able to stretch my definition of love to include *me* in it. If I could learn to ask for help without feeling it was a massive threat to my belonging, without fearing I'd be cast out for being a burden.

I know now that I am not undeserving. I am love. I am loved. Even though I had been unable and unwilling to acknowledge it before, I could see the evidence that pointed to the truth that I was loved for who I was and not what I could offer.

And the same is true for you.

This Is Not Love

Self-abandonment is commonplace. It occurs whenever we question or reject our version of reality in favor of someone else's. When we tell ourselves that wanting or needing something isn't enough to pursue it. This is a survival instinct, and it is conditional love. It is the cruelty of creating a personal definition of enoughness that will never include you as you are. It is rejecting yourself first instead of staying steadfast at your own side.

This cannot stand.

You cannot build a trust-filled relationship with yourself if you are consistently abandoning yourself in the face of disappointment or the presence of your basic human needs. You cannot expect to know what you want and need if you do not take the time to get to know yourself, beyond the relationship-lite version of what is easy or looks good from the outside.

Loving yourself is making the choice each and every day to remain by your own side no matter what. No matter how badly you screw up. No matter how pathetic or inconvenient your needs make you feel. No matter if someone else loves or approves of you. No matter if you are left out, abandoned, unappreciated, betrayed, divorced, or discarded without care. No matter what. Ever.

And if you, like me, read that and wish you could have gotten stuck with anyone but you to do this work with, I resonate.

But what if I were able to stand proudly by my own side instead of being embarrassed by myself? What if instead of focusing on my flaws, I widened my view of myself to include everything I was? Radiant. Strong. Resilient. Fragile. Powerful. Soft. Kind. Funny. Sharp. Impatient. Compassionate.

Picking yourself last is not love. Removing your love in the face of imperfection is not love. Pretending you don't have needs to keep from burdening others is not love. Dropping yourself every time someone comes around asking for your attention is not love. Forcing yourself to produce faster or more than you are humanly able is not love. Shaming yourself for your lack of productivity is not love. Believing you have to shave off parts of yourself, dumb yourself down, or pretend so that you will be accepted is not love. Pretending you don't matter is not love. It is abuse.

This is your invitation to stop offering yourself conditional love and practice enveloping yourself in the unconditional love you ache for. You can have that right this second if you want it, but you have to be willing to pick yourself.

Journal prompts to dive deeper:

What words, actions, or behaviors indicate to you that you are loved?

What words, actions, or behaviors indicate to you that you are not loved?

What does love feel like in your body?

What beliefs or stories do you carry about what it means to be worthy of love?

What grief do you carry from your own experiences with love?

Why do you routinely abandon yourself or deem yourself unlovable?

Unconditional Self-Support

Many of us are confused about unconditional self-love because we have been conditioned to believe it is reserved for someone out there who has met a certain standard for deserving it. This idealized someone is always quite unlike us and out of reach by design, so that we keep working harder in an attempt to meet this unmeetable standard of deserving. At the same time, this conditioning has taught us to be afraid of our own love and to believe that our lives will fall apart if we start to be kind to ourselves. That without all of the rules we have learned and firmly keep in place, we would crumble into nothingness. That without our own cruelty, we would never get anything done. That self-love is analogous to stagnation, lacking the necessary productivity, drive, and growth to be deemed worthy. These beliefs create an inner environment with a significant lack of self-love, and they are rooted in a lack of self-trust. We attempt to rule what we do not trust, and when we do not trust ourselves, our rules for ourselves become essential for continuing our lives as we know them.

However, true self-love is not stagnation. Self-love is caring for yourself as if you are worthy of care, whether or not you believe it in the moment. Self-love is the blossom of a relationship with yourself deeply rooted in trust. It grows through and from appreciation. When you care for yourself this way, it cultivates a safe environment within you, fertile for growth and full expression. This love is a verb. To love yourself. To care for yourself WITH love. To love ON yourself. Right now. As you are.

Take a moment to return to your inner landscape, the wild expanse of land that is your responsibility. Love is caring for the land you have instead of continually comparing your land to the land you've been conditioned to want. Love is the choice to attend to, look after, and cherish your unmanicured, wild self. It is the choice to make peace with the idiosyncrasies of this swath of earth. Maybe your soil is too acidic to grow the type of flower garden you had your mind set on, or the topography isn't suitable for the type of outdoor patio you wanted to build.

Loving yourself means caring for the land you've been given instead of the land you've been conditioned to believe is *right* or *best*. It is the choice to get up each day and water your plants, tenderly dragging your hands through the earth to remove unwanted growth or uproot vestiges of old growth no longer aligned with your needs or vision. It is the choice to hold yourself accountable for showing up, even when you would rather sleep in, numb out, or forfeit your leadership in the face of supreme discomfort.

It is important to acknowledge that this form of self-accountability and gentle discipline is a paradigm shift from what is offered so often in the world around us. There may be many, many people in your life who believe that what is *right* and *best* is to conform and devote your life to competing with the ideal version of you that lives in your mind. Although that is true, you can choose to relate to yourself differently. You do not need anyone's permission to embrace this shift.

In some ways, loving and caring for yourself are more work than scrambling to do all of the *right* and *best* things that ensure your belonging. But your loving and caring actions will be sustainable and sovereign. Your choices will be rooted deeply in your beliefs and values. As your relationships stretch to accommodate you in your fullness, some will break, but the freedom you find in the ones that remain will be worth the hurt. Your life will be yours for the living. This isn't the rom-com love you've been fed, where only the worthy few get to live happily ever after. This love is thick, brave, and unconditional, and you can have it without having to earn it.

Journal prompts to dive deeper:

What are the ways you have tried to earn or ensure love over the course of your life?

How are you currently attempting to earn love?

What do you fear would happen if you stopped working to earn everyone else's love and started cultivating your own?

What do you love about yourself?

Make a list of moments, experiences, big accomplishments, and tiny moments when you showed up for yourself that fill you with pride or self-appreciation.

What would it look like to unconditionally support and care for yourself?

Practice: Saying What You Mean

I say what I mean. I ask for what I need.

When I state an opinion and you tell me I'm wrong, I feel as though there is no room for my truth here.

If I'm really honest, I am afraid to tell you how I feel because I am telling myself the story that you won't love me anymore if I share my truth with you.

I actually prefer to wash my dishes in the morning, with a cup of coffee at my side and NPR on the radio.

I say what I mean. I ask for what I need.

Could you hold me for a minute?

Can we sit next to each other and not say anything?

I have a lot on my plate today. Could you go grocery shopping this evening instead?

I say what I mean. I ask for what I need.

I'm scared. I don't know why.

Today I learned that I'm actually really excited to try _____.

You and I disagree on that point, and that's okay.

I say what I mean. I ask for what I need.

I'm sorry. I can't help you with that today, but how about we get coffee next week?

No.

I'm pouring all of my extra energy into finishing this project right now, so I have to decline.

I say what I mean. I ask for what I need.

I would prefer to eat dinner at home.

I am reminded of my parents when we fight. When I am in that space, I am extra sensitive to feeling criticized.

I need five minutes to collect myself.

I say what I mean. I ask for what I need.

Advocating for your needs is an act of love. Creating boundaries that enable you to fully exist and thrive in your relationships is an act of love. A boundary can be a verbal request about how you would like to be treated, but it could also be an energetic agreement with yourself about what you will and will not tolerate. Over the course of your life, to please others, you may have said yes to things you wanted to say no to. You may have trespassed against yourself to fit the constrictions placed upon you, both imagined and real. It is important to address the imagination here because so often these conversations are unspoken, and in the silence, we are left to assume the worst. You might have avoided setting the boundaries that would enable you to thrive in your relationships because you were never taught you were allowed to.

What if it were possible to reimagine your boundary as a sacred perimeter between where you end and the rest of the world begins? As noted earlier, your boundaries are a permeable border, a fence around your inner and outer landscape. This boundary is strong when you protect yourself the way you would protect something special. It is an expression of your love for your life, so you can be discerning about how you want to use your energy each day. It provides a flexible structure, a reliable shell, to keep you safe and well-tended. This boundary is sturdy so that you can be soft within, without the hypervigilance of the perpetually overextended and undernourished.

To create these boundaries and advocate for what you need, you have to stop making assumptions, expecting other people to read your mind or attempting to read their minds so that you can preemptively please them by fulfilling unstated needs. You have to choose to want to live differently than you have been living. You have to be willing to be uncomfortable as you practice holding yourself accountable, standing in your integrity, and not picking up the hot potatoes.

START HERE

Ask yourself: *Is there a time of day or situation that is causing me stress or making me feel angry or resentful?* If it helps, pull out your journal and do some freewriting with this as a prompt.

After you've gotten clear about the situation where you could use an extra layer of support, start brainstorming what you might want or need to do differently to meet your own needs. Be creative. Tune in to what would feel really good if you could focus only on yourself and meeting your own needs.

Ask yourself: *What would I ask for here if I TRULY felt I could ask for anything?* Tune in to the fullness of what you are aching for before you begin compromising and imagining how that boundary will be received.

Your role in your relationships is to verbalize what you need. Your job is not to micromanage, compromise, or diminish your needs based on whether you think someone will meet that need. Your job is to ask for what you need. Their job is to determine whether they have the capacity at the moment to join you in meeting that need. Your job is to tolerate their response and refuse to judge the validity of your need or abandon yourself based on their response.

If you don't feel ready to share your truth out loud, there is space for you to say what you mean and ask for what you need in your relationship with yourself. Practice giving yourself permission to offer your unvarnished, imperfect truths, holding them gently as you coax more and more truth out of yourself. You do not need to rush to share your truth with anyone just yet. This can be for you and you alone.

THIS MIGHT LOOK LIKE . . .

If you're at the self-responsibility stage, this might look like making a plan to bring more logistical ease to a challenging transition during your day. Ask yourself, "What do I need to feel better supported in this situation?"

If you're at the self-care stage, this might look like widening your scope to think about the lead-up and letdown after a stressful situation. Ask yourself, "How can I better care for myself in the moments leading up to this stressful situation? What do I need afterward to feel seen, held, and heard?"

If you're at the self-trust stage, this might look like reminding yourself that your truth is welcome and that it doesn't have to be perfectly articulated or delivered at just the right moment to matter.

If you're at the self-love stage, this might look like reminding yourself it is your job to have your own back no matter what and getting courageous around asking for what you REALLY want and need from an important relationship, even if that relationship is the one with yourself.

If you are at the advocacy stage, this might look like having a conversation with the humans in your life about the resentment you are feeling and then collaborating to satisfy the needs of both or all parties. Sarah was seven years old when she learned how to hide her needs in an attempt to keep the peace in her home, in particular not to provoke the ire of her mother, who was often overworked and had little capacity for her children's emotions. As an adult, Sarah would find herself resentful of her boyfriend's needs. *How dare he!* she would think to herself when he asked her for a cup of coffee one day. *Doesn't he see how many things I am juggling? He must not love me.* During her upbringing, Sarah had not only learned to bypass her own needs but also had absorbed the belief that loving someone meant not bothering them with your needs. This belief isolated her with her needs and impacted her ability to cultivate intimacy with her boyfriend. "I want to feel free," she said in a session one day. "I want for us to be able to be there for each other without me feeling so angry about it. I also want to be able to receive. I feel like I'm just repeating these patterns from my childhood over and over, where I am too afraid to burden him with my needs and overwhelm him." As she began to unwind these stories, Sarah was able to understand how it wasn't her boyfriend asking for a cup of coffee that was the problem, but what she was making that ask mean, namely that he didn't see her, love her, or appreciate how hard she was working. When she was able to understand her own needs, Sarah was able to let the coffee be just that, a cup of coffee, and ask for the verbal recognition that made her feel truly cherished and loved.

Overdelivering to Earn Love

"Is there anything that you need from me?" I asked.

The first time these words left my lips they felt so foreign. My sister was sick. She was sitting calmly, but everything in me wanted to leap into action, moving quickly in a million ways to do things for her, things she had not yet asked for. She was sick, but at that moment she was already caring for herself. She was simply going through it, and that was painful for me to experience.

At the beginning of every retreat I run, I tell participants I have a vested interest in collaborating with them to meet each and every need they have during the weekend but that they are responsible for asking for what they need. This is a boundary that has been hard-won for me over the course of the last ten years, a boundary that tells both me and the people I'm in relationship with what they can expect from me. Before this boundary, my life was a gnarled tangle of unexpressed desires and boiling resentments. I falsely equated mind reading with love, believing that if those I was in a relationship with really loved me, they would "just know" what I needed and that it was my job to read their minds in return. I spent the majority of my daily energy jumping others' fences and mucking around in their landscapes, attempting to ensure my safety, belonging, and goodness by being the *best* I could be, a goal so often out of reach for my fumbling human self.

Loving someone opens us up to the unmitigated ache of feeling what our loved one feels, often without recourse to take action on their behalf. It hurts to see humans we love in pain, and sometimes we rush to mend and fix in an effort to staunch our pain at seeing their struggle instead of or in addition to helping them. But love also means tolerating another human being's experience and allowing them their spiritual free will and choice. We resist the urge to jump in and instead honor both them and ourselves by holding space. We commit to explicit agreements and do our job, not theirs.

"Is there anything that you need from me?"

She shook her head. Like most healing and growth, this moment was barely a blip in the scheme of my life, but it was the first time I practiced this boundary instead of leaping into my well-worn pattern of overextending myself, which actually would have been an attempt to fix her to quiet my own discomfort and shore up my need for safety.

Journal prompts to dive deeper:

How does mind reading show up in your relationships?

What needs have you been waiting for the people around you to "just know" so that you don't have to directly tell them? Make a list.

Where and how have you been expecting others to overdeliver, overserve, or hop their fence to care for you?

Where and how have you been overdelivering, overserving, or hopping your fence to care for others?

Where and how have you been treating others the way you'd like to be treated, attempting to show them what you desire instead of stating your needs directly?

Loving Yourself by Caring for Yourself
On Purpose and Often

What stories do you carry about what it means to receive love and care? Have you been raised to see your own love as secondary or less than romantic love or the attention of a close friend? Have you lamented the prospect of being left alone with yourself—your lament laced with the bitter suspicion that *better* people don't have to care for themselves because they are surrounded by overflowing love that reflects their magnificence back to them daily? Have you been taught that love means people around you should *just know* exactly what you require and give to you without your raising a finger? (And if they aren't doing that? *Well, you must not be worth it.*)

Loving yourself on purpose is a specific way to respond to yourself with increasing levels of nuance. It is the result of paying close attention to yourself, as you learn what soothes you and urges you to unfurl and bloom as you come alive. You don't have to love everything about yourself to act lovingly toward yourself. An earlier experience of receiving the kind of love you are hungry for is also not a prerequisite for experiencing it now. Loving yourself on purpose and often is the practice of teaching yourself what you require and teaching yourself that you are allowed to receive the love you desire through your daily actions.

An incredible intimacy results when you permit yourself to be cared for (by yourself and others) in precise and deeply supportive ways. Too often we're waiting to become lovable to start receiving this care because we mistakenly assume when we've worked ourselves up to lovability, then love will happen naturally. However, you can create these structures from your deep desire to take better care of yourself and following through with that desire. If you've never before been loved the way you want or need to be loved, you can start right now. And in doing so, you create a blueprint for what you need in your relationships.

Much in this book exists to support you in expanding your vocabulary of what is possible to need. There will be needs that are more easily accessible to you. I refer to this form of care as the linchpin, meaning that it is THE THING that makes everything else feel easier and enables us to operate more smoothly in our bodies and in our lives.

Your linchpin is a core set of needs that, if met, hold things together in a cohesive and good-feeling way. For me, caring for my physical body in a structured way gives me an internal scaffolding to hold my big emotions. Since I was a child, I have felt most cared for when a daily structure is upheld and prioritized. As an adult, I find that emotional and structural consistency is a vital aspect of my relationships. This is not ever the first thing I'd have thought about if you asked me how I need to be loved. But beneath love notes and grand romantic gestures, I am turned on and held close by the intimacy of predictable daily life. When I make sure I move my body, rest, hydrate, eat, and take my vitamins regularly, I feel more shored up and resilient in the face of big feelings.

You also have a primary mode of care like this, a way you most easily, pleasurably, and enjoyably receive care and support that both grounds and stirs you. Here are some examples of how to incorporate your primary mode of care into your relationship with yourself:

Emotional Body

Tending to your emotional needs requires you to be attentive to your most essential, tender, and true self, the self buried beneath the many roles you play each day. What supports you in feeling safe? What in you aches to be seen, held, and nourished? How do you learn to create systems and structures of self-support that enable you to more present and responsive to your feelings?

1. Seek out a dream team of tinctures, balms, and plant medicine allies to nourish and tend to your nervous system. Plant medicines and mineral supplements can support your energetic foundation, giving a greater capacity and deeply felt resilience for managing everything on your plate.

2. Practice speaking to yourself the way someone would who loves you unconditionally might. Remember, this doesn't mean faking it until you make it or bypassing disappointment. Instead, it means giving yourself the benefit of the doubt, lifting yourself up whenever possible, and intentionally speaking to yourself with as much kindness and compassion as you can muster.

3. Hold yourself. Literally. Put a blanket around yourself and hold it tight to swaddle yourself. Rock a little bit if it feels good. Breathe deeply and allow yourself to feel held, secure, and supported for a few minutes.

Physical Body

Tending to your physical body is the realm of daily rituals and routines that support your physical wellness, from flossing your teeth and taking your meds to moving your body and making sure you eat lunch and drink enough water. These pillars of physical strength are often over-looked as something we'll get to someday once we [insert the distraction here]. By honoring your physical needs with consistency, you are tending to your energetic capacity and shoring up your body's stamina for whatever challenge you encounter.

1. Make a plan to feed and hydrate yourself throughout the day. Take time this week to focus on keeping your blood sugar stable by eating at regular intervals. As with tending to any need, start with what is delicious and nourishing.

2. REST. Remember, rest is any activity that fills your cup and restores your energy. If you're getting stuck with this, refer back to the chapter on rest.

3. Complete a stress cycle every day. A stress cycle begins with a stressor—like navigating conflict in a relationship, receiving harsh feedback, or encountering a trauma trigger—which

then activates a physiological response of fight, flight, fawn, or freeze. Our heart races, breathing quickens, muscles tense, and our bodies release stress hormones. In nature, we might run away and find a safe place to rest after such an encounter. This burst of activity followed by rest completes the stress response cycle and allows us to recover. But we don't always complete our stress cycles in modern life, which drains us. A few strategies for completing stress cycles are physical activity, creativity, laughing, crying, physical affection, and deep breathing. It doesn't have to be fancy. Dance around your kitchen, doodle, watch a favorite TV show that cracks you up, scream-sing in the car along with your favorite songs, hug someone for at least twenty seconds, or pet your dog or cat.

Mental Body

Tending to your mental body and cultivating self-trust asks us to make a daily practice of self-kindness, compassionate self-talk, and prioritizing whatever creates space and calm in our inner landscape. By bringing our attention to our inner world, we are able to partner with ourselves and stand by our own side during times of mental stress or anxiety.

1. Create headspace by pulling out a big piece of white paper and writing down everything you've been carrying with you, however big or small. Use the page to help you hold everything you are currently grappling with. Once these things are out of your head and onto the page, you will be better able to make sense of it all, and WHEW! it will feel better laying that heavy burden down too.

2. Set boundaries with yourself and others. It can be tempting to push your needs to the side to keep saying yes, but hear me when I tell you that **nothing** in your life works if you are not in good working order, which includes being well-rested and well-nourished.

3. Get sensory rest. You are navigating a profound amount of
   sensory input on a daily basis—the sounds, smells, visual stimuli,
   tastes, and physical sensations that fill your waking hours to the
   brim. Give yourself sensory rest by secluding yourself in a room,
   such as a bathroom, turning off the light, and covering your ears
   for a couple of minutes. Or lie down with a lavender pillow or
   T-shirt over your eyes for a few minutes. Drive in silence instead
   of listening to the news. Bathe in the dark to rest your eyes. A
   little of this goes a very long way.

Spiritual Body

Tending to your spiritual need for connection and belonging is both an
individual and a collective need. As you reorient yourself toward your
own belonging, remember that these actions are exactly that, a reorientation. Give yourself permission to curl up in your own lap when you
are needy, grief-stricken, confused, overwhelmed, or sad. Connect with
the people and things in the world that help you feel like the truest, most
fully expressed version of yourself.

1. Too often we prioritize connecting with others through
   technology over connecting with ourselves, only to realize
   that scrolling through social media (again) doesn't actually
   make us feel all that connected. Experiment with creating
   some boundaries with your technology use as another way
   to give yourself rest from visual stimuli and other people's
   opinions. These boundaries might include social media,
   email, the news, online gaming, and anything else you notice
   you could use a break from.

2. Create a phenology wheel—a way to cultivate intimacy with
   the natural world around you is to track the moon cycle, tides,
   weather, or the growth cycle of plants indigenous to your area.
   A phenology wheel is a circle divided into sections where you
   record your observations of the natural world. You might use it

to track the changes in your garden over the course of the year, or the moon's cycles, or the weather throughout the seasons.

3. Gather and connect with the humans in your life by reaching out and getting people together, whether for an informal hangout or a more formal gathering like a party or a meal. As you consider the plan for your gathering, connect with yourself first before connecting with others. Get curious about how you are feeling and what you hope to get out of the gathering.

Energetic Body

Meeting your energetic needs includes you becoming a detective of your experiences and communicating with yourself honestly to create better-fitting experiences for yourself in the future. Remember, these will be unique to you; there's no need to force yourself into a cookie-cutter experience. Surround yourself with any stimuli that works for your body—words, images, colors, textures, scents, tastes, and sounds that energize you and make you feel more like yourself.

1. Go back to the list you made earlier of what lights you up. This is a running list, so please add to it as you move through your life. I guarantee you that half of the activities on your list won't live up to your expectations, but some of them will.

2. Devote yourself to bringing an ounce more pleasure, joy, and YOU to any given moment. This prompt is one of my favorites, inspired by the work of Ann Nguyen and Anna Guest-Jelley. I love it because of how deliciously doable it feels. You don't have to change it ALL. You just have to think about what might make this moment just a touch more enjoyable. A warm pair of socks. A fresh glass of water. A shower. A different radio station. A blanket for my lap. To get up and walk outside for ten minutes. An orgasm. A more comfortable pair of underwear. A hot cup of coffee or tea. The perfect piece of toast. It doesn't have to be complicated or earth-shattering to feel really, really good. Take a

moment now to ask yourself how you can bring a little bit more pleasure and ease into this moment.

3. Fill your feed. Whom you choose to follow, absorb, read, and connect with online has an enormous impact on your creativity and perspective each day, which is why a glorious practice for tending to your need for inspiration is to fill your feed with people who inspire you. Is there a particular edge you are leaning into at the moment? How can you surround yourself with support for that?

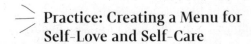

Practice: Creating a Menu for Self-Love and Self-Care

START HERE

Pull out your journal and ask yourself the following questions:

Over the course of my life, what has soothed me when I was upset or ungrounded?

Knowing what I need to feel better, what brings me alive when I am stuck or having a hard time?

Using your notes from the writing exercises and the modes of care described above, I encourage you to create two short menus for your care: one for moments when you need soothing and grounding, and the other for when you are aching to bloom again and come alive through consistent loving care.

These menus will prove infinitely useful when you are edging into a care crisis. Use them in conjunction with the warning-signs practice to work on seeing a care crisis approaching from a further and further distance so that you can care for yourself proactively instead of reactively. These lists are meant to be living documents, so update them, adding and tailoring with increasing levels of nuance and specificity as you gain more information about yourself in different situations.

THIS MIGHT LOOK LIKE . . .

If you're at the self-responsibility stage, this might look like using this tool to identify what mode of care makes the biggest impact on the felt experience of your daily life.

If you're at the self-care stage, this might look like brainstorming new and increasingly nuanced ways to meet your primary care needs.

If you're at the self-trust stage, this might look like folding your primary mode of care into your life EVERY day and not just when you notice you are in need, because it feels good to be cared for this way.

If you're at the self-love stage, this might look like remembering you are unique. The way you most easily and comfortably receive love is unique, and the more you can tend to your need for love in increasingly specific and good-feeling ways, the more data you will have to share with others about how you desire to be treated.

If you are at the advocacy stage, this might look like inviting others into your primary mode of care by sharing your menus with others as you advocate for your love needs in your relationships.

I Love You, but I Don't Like You Right Now

I remember the soft thud the first time I really heard it: *I love you, but I don't like you right now.* The energy of it rippled through my body, the very idea of a love so vast it could accommodate dislike, disappointment, mistrust, anger, frustration, and grief. This love was flexible enough to encompass multifaceted truth. It felt safe in its steadfast permanence. There was nothing this love could not make space to repair.

Even as I started to realize that this was the love I offered those closest to me, I felt stunned that this was an option available to me. Why have I been telling myself love isn't possible here? Is it possible to trust that even a series of infractions aren't enough to topple the totality of what I've built?

I love you, but I don't like you right now.

This is soft, flexible love. Brave love. The kind of love that sustains disruption and upset, growing and adapting as it becomes. How long had I been living under the threat and panic of having everything taken away? My love. My belonging. My life. I was stunned to realize how hard I had been working, overdelivering to earn MY OWN love as much as anyone else's.

I was stunned to realize that I had been quick to pull my love away as I punished myself for my inadequacies with every perceived fumble or failure. That I expected other people to leave me when I screwed up because this was when I left *myself*. That I fed myself only the crumbs that were left over after I was done loving everyone else into wholeness. That without a substantial change in my approach to my relationship with myself, I would never feel whole because I was subsisting on chaos and unreliability.

This was the piece that no one else could do for me, and this is the piece I cannot do for you. No one else could decide I was worthy of my own love, that I could build my belonging on the understanding that I am a person who sometimes does disappointing or frustrating things, and that the legacy of trust I am building has to include my ability to respond to disappointment if it is going to be whole. *I love you, but I don't like you right now.* This love is permanent. There is nothing I can do to make me take away my love. There is nothing for me to earn here.

I am sovereign as I grant and grow my own love. This love is my greatest wish for you: to love yourself in such an expansive and dynamic way that there is room for everything that you are.

Commitments to My Need for Love

— We tend to think of love as a feeling. It's not. It's a decision. Choosing to love myself is the necessary risk of unlearning everything I've been taught about who and how I should be to connect with who I am and how I feel.

— There's a lot of talk about self-love as something you achieve. This is not true. Loving myself is making the choice every day, every moment, to remain by my own side no matter what. Even when I am not "lovable." I can love myself even when I don't like myself in a given moment, offering myself the grace of knowing I do not need to be perfect to be worthy of love.

— I deserve unconditional self-love right now. Not "someday." Not when I earn it. Right now. As I am. Unconditional self-love is acting in ways that tend to my inner landscape and loving what is, not what could be or what someone else has.

— Saying what I mean and asking for what I need are huge acts of love, as is knowing my boundaries. If I have a habit of overdelivering to earn love, I've got some work to do here.

CHAPTER 9

Belonging

BLESSING

I belong. My belonging belongs to me.

I am responsible for cultivating my own unconditional love. I am responsible for ensuring my own safety and refusing to abandon myself no matter how unsafe my circumstances feel or become. I am responsible for fully embodying my role as the tender steward of my life.

I belong. My belonging belongs to me.

I don't need anyone to approve of me for me to be deemed worthy or whole.

I have been trained to prefer and trust external sources of validation over trusting myself. I liberate myself by stepping into this knowing: no one can ever take away my belonging.

Even as I think this, my wounds sputter in disbelief.

But it happened before.

But I will be lost if they leave me.

But what if I trust myself and allow myself to be vulnerable, and no one accepts me?

I walk the length of my life and collect the splintered and wounded parts of myself. I cradle my pain in my capable hands. I welcome these wounded parts back into my fullness and commit to a wholeness that has always been inconvenient and deeply human. I teach myself what it means to be seen, held, and unconditionally regarded as worthy of my own care.

I remind myself that I don't need anyone else's permission to be who I already am. I don't need anyone to approve of me in order for me to be enough. If they are willing to leave me for being myself, then they are already gone, even if I am unable or unwilling to see it.

When I am unsteady, I lean into the possibility that there is at least as much right about me as there is wrong. I am learning to trust the brilliance of my own missteps. I resist the urge to judge myself and learn to approach myself with curiosity and creativity instead. I am teaching myself a new way of showing up in the world, moment by moment and step by step.

My belonging belongs to me.

I HAD AN EPIPHANY while walking across my college campus at 3:00 a.m., but it certainly wasn't the one that I was hoping for. I had been "working" on my self-love for so long, caught between making myself into someone more socially valuable and knowing I had to figure out how to belong to myself first. But really, I was waiting for a magical moment when it would feel easier, when I would be permanently buoyed by a profound sense of self-adoration and magically take responsibility for myself. Instead of protecting and caring for myself, I had made a habit out of outsourcing my worthiness, handing myself over for inspection and validation.

It was after a late-night party during my freshman year at college. I had gone out in my most hopeful outfit, as I often did, dressing myself up in a mix of self-loathing and wishing someone somewhere would scoop me up and make me feel worthy for the night. Growing up, I was the secret girl. The closet girl. The girl you pretended to be ashamed of kissing. The girl you hooked up with and lied about to your friends afterward. I longed to feel chosen and cherished, but I often found my way into untrustworthy hands, hands that hurt, hands that helped me believe the story that I should just take what I could get and feel lucky about it. This night was very similar. I allowed someone to take me home, but the minute I got there I wanted to leave. I felt guilty about my lack of interest. I told myself that tired story that I should feel lucky to receive his attention and that I owed him something for it. I told myself that the most convenient route from point A (standing in his room) to point B (walking out the door) was to pass through his bed. After all, he went through all the effort of talking to me for an hour. It didn't mean that much to me. So I made myself small and crawled into the dark place at the back of my brain that was cozy and familiar. At 3:00 a.m., I collected that hopeful outfit, dressed myself, and walked across campus, glancing through anxious text messages from my roommate and struggling to light a cigarette with shaking hands.

What struck me was how familiar it all felt. The furtive hands behind closed doors. The secrecy. The hope that this time I might matter. The way that I routinely abandoned myself in an attempt to belong. The distinct lack of care when I tried to earn my worth by sleeping with people who didn't respect or revere me. Their attitudes toward me mirrored reflections of my own feelings about myself.

> I can't keep living this way. If I keep living this
> way, I will die this way—not mattering to myself
> or believing I am worthy of my own care.

And suddenly, it wasn't just that moment but also the heartbreaking incident when I had been so weak from that diet I couldn't walk up the four flights of stairs to my dorm room. It was also the many, many moments when I punished myself for being too much, skewering myself with private vitriol for never ever measuring up to the ideals of beauty and worth I carried in me. It was all of the moments prior, with similar boys, when I had made similar choices and thought I deserved to use myself to get ahead.

> I can't keep living this way, a stranger in my own
> body, an enemy to myself. I can't keep living
> this way. I have to start taking responsibility
> for what is mine to protect and stand up for.

> ### Journal prompts to dive deeper:
>
> What words, actions, or behaviors signal to you that you belong?
>
> What words, actions, or behaviors signal to you that you do not belong?
>
> What does it mean to belong?
>
> What does belonging feel like in your body?
>
> What beliefs, stories, or feelings do you carry about your experiences with belonging?

Why Do You Trespass Against Yourself?

You trespass against yourself in each moment that you forfeit your true nature in favor of the carefully curated existence you deem necessary to ensure your belonging. It is the belief or untested suspicion that who and how you are aren't worthy of love. You hide your needs. Say you're fine when you're not. Say yes before you check in with yourself to find out what you really want and need.

Each moment of self-abandonment takes us further away from deepening into the trust, safety, and intimacy of belonging to ourselves, exactly as we are. Each time we prioritize someone else's knowledge over our own or look outside ourselves for what is *right* or *best* to do, we trespass against our own belonging. This doesn't mean that other people don't exist for us, though it does mean we can and should turn to ourselves first before looking outside ourselves for guidance. True belonging is rooted in creating expansive space for everything that we are inside our relationship with ourselves—the good, the bad, and the in-between. It is the commitment to be in relationship with ourselves no matter who we are joined by or what circumstances surround us.

When we struggle to establish boundaries with ourselves, it is because at some point in our lives we absorbed the message that we needed to be unendingly available to others to keep ourselves safe and ensure our belonging in our families, communities, workplaces, and friend circles. Either directly or indirectly, we learned the rules of what was and was not permitted, and we began conforming to those rules to keep ourselves safe. When we are small children, this is necessary to ensure our safety, since our very existence depends on our ability to belong to our caregivers. We learn to associate our "goodness" (i.e., how well we fit their norms) with getting our basic needs met. Because of our young age, these rules are encoded without nuance, and they grow into all-or-nothing thinking by adulthood. This all-or-nothing thinking manifests in hard boundaries around what is *good* and what is *bad*, with very little flexibility or space for expansion. For example, if I do something disappointing or fail at something I try to achieve, it is not *just* disappointing—I am disappointing. It's not just a failure; I am a failure by proxy. Conversely, I cannot be good unless I am ALL good, perfect in every way—acing every test that comes my way and looking great while doing it. We swing back and forth between these polarities and more often than not relegate ourselves to the "bad" category at the sight of any perceived flaw.

We all have flaws. But we are not all bad (or all good). In fact, most of us are a delightful mixed bag, which is why the nuance required to give ourselves grace is such a powerful practice.

Journal prompts to dive deeper:

When and how do you trespass against belonging to yourself in favor of belonging to your community or relationships?

What are the circumstances, situations, or relationships where you struggle to belong to yourself the most?

What would be possible for you if you felt as though you belonged without having to earn it?

What would belonging to yourself first look like? What would you do differently?

What are your fears around belonging to yourself first?

What Are You Ready, Able, and Willing to Forgive Yourself For?

Forgiveness is integral to belonging. You might avoid or resist forgiveness because, like love, you associate it with stagnation. You might wonder whether you will cease growing or showing up for yourself if you forgive yourself for your perceived flaws. You might wonder how you will incentivize yourself for the positive change you seek in your life if you surrender your beloved coping mechanisms of shame and ridicule.

Forgiveness is not stagnating. It is life-generating. Belonging to yourself requires you to crawl into the cracks in your relationship with yourself and pour your love where you hurt the most. We are tending to our wounds as we heal our own beliefs around who and how we have to be to belong. Forgiveness reminds us that we do not have to feel we deserve belonging to get it. Who you have been is a part of who you are, but it does not wholly define you. Forgiveness is the decision to move forward in tender stewardship and active participation. You are awake, aware, present, and sovereign now.

Ask yourself: What am I ready, able, and willing to forgive myself for?

The mistakes. The overdraft fees. The missed
opportunities. The shitty behavior. The moments
you disappointed yourself by being utterly, messily,
and undeniably human. The perceived failures. The
time(s) you let yourself or someone else down.
The huge mistakes you relive daily. The moments
of self-sabotage and hiding from your needs.

Grant yourself the grace of a blank page and a clean start. Write down everything that comes to mind, breathing deeply and reminding yourself that these moments in time are a part of you but they do not wholly define you. You are neither wholly good nor wholly bad. You are spectacularly human.

Belonging to Yourself First

As you reorient yourself toward your own belonging, remember that these actions are indeed a reorientation. Give yourself permission to unravel within your expansive inner landscape. Resource yourself for this self-inquiry and take your whole body with you as you stretch to accommodate all that you are. Honor your needs as they arise. With all of these actions, you are reinforcing a powerful new message to yourself: *I see you. I accept you. I will keep you safe. I love you.* This belonging is no longer attached to a lengthy list of rules about who or what is required of you to ensure it. This way of being is reinforced through daily action. This is not work you can do once and then put on a shelf. We live in a world that is continually sending us messages about what is right and good to do or be, so we must be equally consistent in our conscious choice to remain by our own side.

Tangibly belonging to yourself on a daily basis might look like the choice to prioritize your essential self-care, holding those moments, rituals, and practices as sacred no matter what else is happening in your life or who requires your attention. It is found in the choice to continue questioning, in the lifelong allegiance to yourself first and foremost.

Start by listing a handful of specific situations, circumstances, or relationships where you notice yourself routinely trespassing against yourself. You might choose to pull out a piece of paper and write these specifics down in list form. Then, on the other side of the paper, start brainstorming how you wish you would respond in those situations or how you might like to respond differently next time.

When setting the intention to belong to myself more readily, I find it useful to think about who I turn to for my most important questions. When left unattended, this position in my life is occupied by the faceless choir of voices I have accumulated from the bullies I've encountered, society at large, the media, and the people who have hurt me the worst. When I turn toward this faceless choir, I routinely prioritize their opinions and voices over my own. This repeated pattern of looking outside myself for information is a vestige of a safety practice I grew up with, which is rooted in the belief that other people's opinions are more valuable than my own and that a "good decision" is one that everyone in the world agrees on. (This was an impossible task, but I spent ample energy striving for it nonetheless.)

In my desire to belong to myself, I imagine turning away from the faceless choir and toward myself, centering my own thoughts, feelings, desires, and needs. This doesn't mean other people's voices, thoughts, or opinions cease to exist, but that the new natural order is they are second to my own voice, thoughts, and opinions. This is what it means to be in right relationship with myself. It means I am the sovereign leader, tender steward, and gatekeeper of my own life. I am no longer interested in having my self-image defined by a world that cannot know or appreciate me. I am no longer interested in embodying or perpetuating the fatphobia or homophobia as it relates to me or the racism, ableism, ageism, or transphobia as they relate to my values or those whom I love. I reclaim the thoughts, opinions, and voices that occupy the center of my life and inform my choices. This is an active choice to stand by my own humanity, even in the face of a world that is not aligned with my values. I will keep myself safe by choosing where and how to divest from the world's messages, knowing there are sacrifices and risks to confronting these systems.

Practice: Wheel of the Year

As you have learned by now, the most crucial aspect of honoring your needs is knowing what you actually need to begin with, even and especially if the person you are asking is yourself. The wheel of the year practice is a very practical application for that investigation. As noted earlier, our needs change with time, circumstances, and surroundings. This isn't static work. Our needs are constantly evolving, and one of the best ways we can support ourselves in meeting our needs is to pay attention to them over the span of our lifetimes.

The wheel of the year enables you to tend to yourself compassionately and consistently over the course of the year, reinforcing the knowing that you are not energetically available in the same way each day or each season. Like the tide, your energy will ebb and flow. Like the moon, your energy will wax and wane. You are a human and not a robot, and as such you will not be universally available to produce or create at the same rate each day all year round. This isn't indicative of a personal weakness or a flaw; it is quite literally what it means to exist in a human body. Knowing this about yourself enables you to finally break free from the belief that there is something wrong with you; instead, you can tap into embracing your true nature as a living, breathing sentient being.

START HERE

There are several ways to go about creating your wheel of the year. Choose a path forward that feels good and creatively interesting for you. There is absolutely no wrong way to do this activity. I find it most useful to break the year into seasonal quarters, but you might prefer to break it down monthly or to mark the passage of time by noting important holidays or annual milestones.

Create a physical wheel to fill in by pulling out a huge piece of paper and drawing a big circle on it. Create four quadrants and write the name of a season in each one.

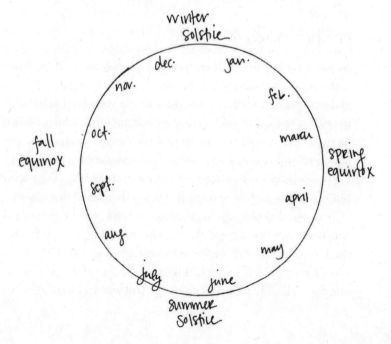

Use the following questions to freewrite about your personal experience with each season, gathering data about yourself. Remember, there is no wrong way to do this. Track and write down anything that feels important to you while trying not to second-guess or censor yourself.

What have I noticed about my energy during previous X seasons? What about my energy during the holidays in this season?

What grief anniversaries of past experiences do I want to pay attention to or hold space for during X season?

If I were to take really good care of myself during X season, what might I keep in mind, watch out for, or plan for in advance?

As you accumulate this data about yourself, distill it down to its most important points. You may want to pull out a second different-colored pen or marker to underline or highlight the most resonant words and ideas.

When you are ready, move on to the next season, and ask the questions again. After you've answered the questions for all four seasons, take your information and plot it out on your wheel of the year by season and month. I like to use a different-colored marker for notes related to each of these sections: energy level, anniversaries and important dates, extra support, and seasonal self-care.

Once you've finished your wheel of the year, keep your chart nearby and refer to it often. Use it to anticipate your needs from a distance, preparing for them before they arrive. Amend this document whenever you unearth a new truth about yourself or make a new discovery about your needs. Let your wheel of the year become a document of seasonal care instructions that support your desire to be a tender steward of your life.

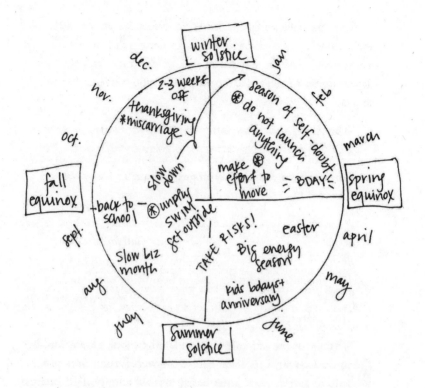

MONTHLY CHECK-INS AND FUTURE PLANNING

An additional practice you might want to incorporate is to set a date with yourself on the first day of every month to review the month that just came to a close and make plans for the month ahead.

Use this check-in to add things from the month that has just ended to your wheel of tending, while they are fresh in your mind. Ask yourself the following questions:

— What worked or didn't work last month?

— What was my energy like?

— What do I want to remember or plan for next year?

Now turn your attention to the month ahead, and ask yourself these questions:

— What do I need to plan for this month?

— What support do I anticipate needing? What is the plan for connecting with that support?

— What do I need to block out or schedule in this month to help me tend to myself with greater ease?

THIS MIGHT LOOK LIKE . . .

If you're at the self-responsibility stage, this might look like checking your wheel at the beginning of the month and planning your self-care and dates to pay attention to in your planner.

If you're at the self-care stage, this might look like seasonally updating your supplements, go-to food choices, movement rituals, and daily routines based on how your body feels and what might be most supportive in the season ahead.

If you're at the self-trust stage, this might look like allowing yourself to deeply rest, because you know in your bones that with time your natural enthusiasm for taking action on what matters most will return.

If you're at the self-love stage, this might look like tending to a working understanding of your own energy rhythm over the arc of the year by using it to make plans, organize creative endeavors, and most importantly cultivate a deep reverence for your body.

If you're at the advocacy stage, this might look like creating boundaries for experiences or events based on your unique needs. Sally used her wheel of the year to completely revamp her plan for the holiday season after realizing that late November and early December are a time of multiple grief anniversaries. Before this, she always made big plans to spend time with family, concoct the perfect holidays for her children, and attend every party she was invited to, but she often felt incredibly fragile and exhausted by mid-December. Sally had been unwittingly muscling through her big grief feelings, believing she could feel them later, at a more convenient time, once the revelry was over. Doing this year after year led to her resenting every holiday obligation, picking fights with her spouse, and feeling more frustrated by every expectation. When she carved out more space for herself in between events and became more selective about what she committed to, she was not only able to create a holiday season that felt much more manageable but also to participate more joyfully in the opportunities for connection she said yes to.

Remember, as with all the practices in this book, your wheel can only support you if you actively interact with it. It cannot help you if you tuck it away in a deep drawer to languish with your IKEA Allen wrenches and rubber bands. Keep your wheel front and center, using it as a tool to get to know yourself on a deep, energetic level so that you can care for yourself in better and better ways each year.

Hiding Stories and What It Means to Take Up Space

I pressed my body against the wall. It was the middle of the night. As an adult now, I know that I was safe, but as an anxious kid, I would lie awake thinking, *What if someone breaks into our house while we are sleeping?* The question curled underneath the door like smoke spilling into the room whenever it was dark and I was the only one awake. *What if I'm not safe?* I practiced hiding by pressing my body into the space between the bed and the wall. Quietly moving inch by inch, I practiced not making a sound while I slid into my hiding spot. I became good at hiding. Being good at hiding meant that I could keep myself safe from any predator who might prowl through my house late at night. I couldn't be in control of that. I could only control how well I concealed myself.

For me, hiding and wanting to be found have always been linked. When I hid as a child, what I desperately wanted was for my parents to wake up and magically know I needed them to find and comfort me. It was the ultimate test of my adolescent worthiness. Would I be found? Was I worth seeking out? Did someone love me enough to notice that I had gone missing? This was a pattern I found myself playing out years later with my partner. Would they come find me when I abandoned myself? Would they notice when I was diminishing or withholding my needs and remind me that I didn't need to do that to receive their love? Did they love me enough to notice that I had gotten lost again in my own dark web of conditions for belonging? Like all such patterns, this one had deep roots.

Believing you are allowed to take up space—physically, mentally, emotionally—is deeply emotional, a complex configuration of fear, yearning, and social conditioning. It involves the part of you that wants to keep you safe by curling into yourself, making you as physically and energetically small as you can. It is also found in the choice not to raise your hand in a meeting or tell the person you love when they've disappointed you. The question about whether you are worthy of taking up space is born from a belief that there is something so deeply flawed about you that you must apologize for it by making it as easy as possible for others to be around you. It is the complete disavowal of your bright spirit and unique light. When we hide in this way, we deliver the message, again and again, that we are not worthy of the same physical and emotional space that others seem to occupy with ease.

As I grew up, I continued to hide with the same fervor I once poured into tucking myself between the bed and the wall at night. I made a habit out of keeping myself small. I hunched over, chin to chest, chest to knees. I wore dark colors—*colors that were flattering for a person of my size*. I pinched my legs together. I sat on my hands. I practiced keeping myself as contained as possible. There was no strength behind my voice. My statements were frequently couched with polite phrases like, "Well, it's only my opinion but . . ." or "Maybe if you approached it from this angle—BUT I could be wrong, of course."

I did not feel that I deserved attention, even as I secretly hungered for it. I felt ashamed for being so big, and not just big in my body but also big in that my thoughts were so expansive they threatened my carefully curated persona, and my ambition was even more gigantic. Believing that my needs were embarrassingly complicated and difficult, I refused to advocate for them to protect myself from becoming a burden to those around me. I preferred the discomfort of not having my needs met to the emotional risk and turmoil of asking for what I needed. In refusing to take up space, I unwittingly reinforced the idea that I was so unwieldy and complicated no one would bother to continue being in relationship with me if they truly knew me. I routinely abandoned myself before I could be abandoned.

Not allowing ourselves to take up space is one of the quietest ways we undermine ourselves on a daily basis. It can feel like a foregone conclusion that you must shrink yourself to belong. But at some point, we must realize that we are harming ourselves with all that hiding. By allowing ourselves only so much ground to stand on, we are denying the full breadth of our beautiful spirits. At some point we begin to ask ourselves: *Is it possible that I am worth more than this? Is it possible that I am worth the inconvenience and special attention I eagerly give to others? Is it selfish to want to feel radiant?*

Taking up space is an act of bravery. At some point, I had to decide I would no longer make myself small or wait for someone else to come and find me. I could no longer expect the humans around me to intervene when I diminished or abandoned myself, coaxing me out of my hiding places. I could no longer be willing to lie awake, tucking myself away between the bed and the wall, waiting. Now I ask for the comfort I need. I am no longer willing to pretend I don't have needs or to reject my humanity for the sake of progress, convenience, or being tolerated. My needs are an indisputable truth of my existence. I am no longer willing to squeeze myself into relationships or situations I have outgrown. I risk the consequence of showing up as I am. I am no longer willing to wait for an invitation to share my fullness with the humans around me or to believe doing so is a risk to my belonging. I belong to myself now.

Practice: Embracing Your Muchness

What would it mean to fully embody your role as the one person in the world who you could never be too much for? What would you accept about yourself? What feelings would you learn to validate, soothe, and hold? What gifts would you give to yourself to encourage your full-throttled expression of self? How might you coax these precious and burdensome aspects of your being out of hiding and give them permission to exist in the bright light of day? What resources or nourishment would you ask yourself for? What would you say without apology or doublespeak?

Belonging to yourself means devoting yourself to remaining present at your own side. It is a commitment to your fullest expression, particularly in your relationship with yourself. It is found by unlearning false beliefs about who and how you have to be to belong and by reclaiming the power of your own ability to hold your many parts.

Depending on the current state of your relationship with yourself, you might need this reminder many, many times. This, too, is a function of your relationship with yourself. You can choose to be generous with your reminders. You are the one who gets to choose, cheer, unearth, and validate.

This practice is to embrace one facet of your much-ness, your fullest expression of self. Implicit in this practice is the choice to allow, accept, and include parts of yourself that other people may have found overwhelming or unacceptable in the past. Devoting yourself to yourself is a brave act, oozing with belonging. You do not need to ask anyone's permission to do this. You do not need to wait for external approval or validation to approve of yourself.

You do not need forgiveness from that person you let down or your father to finally understand you.

You are already equipped with the only thing you need—a deep desire to belong and a readiness to support yourself in whatever way you need.

START HERE

This practice is a bit of a choose-your-own-adventure invitation because you are the only one who truly knows what part of you is aching to belong.

Pull out your journal and ask yourself: *What part of me is aching to belong?*

Do you long to be heard? Seen? Touched? Held?

Do you long for someone to wrap their arms around you and tell you they completely understand?

Do you wish someone would listen without rushing in to fix you?

Do you wish someone would tend to you sweetly, showing you are precious to them?

Do you wish for someone to buoy you up with words of affirmation?

Do you ache for someone else to buy you that exact perfect thing you've been eyeing?

Are you waiting for someone to appreciate you for the effort you've been putting in and thank you?

How can you give yourself **that thing**? How can you make a habit out of turning to yourself to ask what part of you is aching to belong and learn to prioritize the answers you receive?

This belonging might look different from what you were expecting or hoping for. Everything in you might hop up to tell you that you couldn't possibly do this for yourself. If you are feeling this way, be with those feelings. Give yourself permission to feel however you feel, honoring and validating whatever story arises. This is belonging to yourself too. Make space in your relationship with yourself for whatever is true for you right now, and know that rebuilding your relationship with yourself isn't an academic process. It is a fierce commitment to who and how you are, even when you don't like it or wish it were different. Tend to your need for belonging by embracing your *muchness*.

This is tender work, and it does not require you to wait until it gets easy. The wounds you carry around belonging might be profound, but your belonging is not on hold until those wounds are healed. Healing is not a journey with a destination. It is the practice of deepening into your self-responsibility and self-stewardship. Your care must be multifaceted and continuous, not to fix what is broken in you but to love your most tender parts.

You belong to yourself when you attend to your need for water. Or when you say one true, uncensored thing. Or when you ask for what you need, even if you struggle to find your voice or tears run down your face. You belong to yourself when you allow yourself to be where and how you are, even if it is uncomfortable. Belonging is not a magical place where everything is great. It is the continued actions on your own behalf to feed your hunger, prioritize what feels true, TAKE UP SPACE, and have the courage to tell yourself the truth about what you need to thrive.

THIS MIGHT LOOK LIKE . . .

If you're at the self-responsibility stage, this might look like reassuring yourself that you are allowed to want and need what you want and need. Having requirements or desires does not make you too much or too needy. It makes you human.

If you're at the self-care stage, this might look like giving yourself more than the bare minimum, giving yourself more rest, space, hydration, nourishment, pleasure, sex, time outside, or play than you explicitly need to survive.

If you're at the self-trust stage, this might look like becoming more aware of patterns, circumstances, and relationships that trigger your feeling as though you are too much or not enough. What might be happening here? What do you need?

If you're at the self-love stage, this might look like tending to the feelings that surface in the midst of conflict or whenever you feel particularly vulnerable to rejection. How can you stand by your own side and hold your own hand during these moments when you could really use a friend who gets you and adores you unconditionally?

If you're at the advocacy stage, this might look like finding safe pockets of connection to invite your muchness into your relationships with others. Wear the thing. Say the thing. Ask for the thing. Choose the people in your life who you feel most comfortable with and begin experimenting. Remind yourself that your truest self is welcome in those moments and get curious about what that might look and feel like for you.

Commitments to My Need for Belonging

— Belonging is an inside job. By honoring my needs, values, priorities, and desires, I make the choice to belong to myself, even as I exist in a world that tells me I don't matter or should be constantly working to better myself.

— I might have learned to trespass against myself in an effort to belong, hiding my needs, saying yes when I meant no, ignoring my body. But each act of self-abandonment takes me even further away from belonging.

— To move back to self-belonging, I have to start by forgiving myself, even if I have been conditioned to believe I don't deserve this forgiveness. Forgiving myself for what I've done and who I have been is an act of creation that moves me closer to sovereignty.

— One beautiful way of fostering belonging with myself is to attend to my wheel of the year and check in with myself on a regular basis.

— When I am struggling to take up space, I will remind myself that fully embodying my life is my birthright. I am allowed to embrace my muchness and seek out communities and connections where I feel safe to fully express myself.

CHAPTER 10

Celebration

BLESSING

I am cherished.

I choose what and how to celebrate.

I determine my worthiness for celebration, and I am generous with those determinations.

This celebration is intentional. It is a reclamation of space. It is a revolution of spirit.

I meet this need because it generates life within me, even when my conditioning tells me this is the wrong time to celebrate or my celebrations are baseless, frivolous, or unnecessary.

I choose what is deserving of celebration, and I will stretch that definition in my mind to include my perfect and imperfect self. I deliberately witness and lift up everything that is right about me right now, including the things I am conditioned to want to hide or loathe.

I relish in these pleasure-drenched declarations. I resist the story that I am too stuck, mixed-up, or messy to celebrate. I allow my celebrations to be imperfect, as I am. Instead of my messiness disqualifying me from receiving the bounty of my own affection, I choose to rejoice in my shortcomings.

I rejoice in the bravery it takes to show up and fail.

I rejoice in the moments I cared enough to be cautious.

I rejoice in the lessons my perceived laziness teaches me about my need for rest.

I rejoice knowing that I am imperfect—just like every other human, plant, and animal on this planet—and that it is my imperfection that gains me entry into the family of things.

I acknowledge the full breadth of my humanity and honor all I bring to the table. I am aware, now, that perfectionism has taught me to bypass my innate, wild brilliance and to sacrifice the divine knowing of my most fully expressed self.

I do not need to take the seductive invitation my perfectionism offers me—the invitation to suppress everything I have learned about my "unworthy" or "unlovable" parts—in favor of a highly curated expression of self.

I choose to lift up my humanity instead.

I choose to show up as I am wherever and whenever I feel safe to do so.

Embracing these very choices is a celebration in and of itself, as I learn to revel in being myself, out loud and on purpose.

"WAIT—WAS THIS A GIFT?" I spend time daily cultivating my celebrations, getting as specific as possible about the things I love in order to construct moments of time filled with these curated pleasures. The more I get to know myself, the more easily these celebrations come—and the more joyful they have been to receive.

A favorite cake. A night at a hotel I've been
following on Instagram for years. A gift I
earmarked for a special occasion. Time alone.
A beloved walk. A perfect cup of coffee.

But this specific day was one of my favorite celebrations in memory. My partner, Cookie, and I were at our favorite cafe for lunch on my birthday. The food was, as always, delicious, but the conversation was incredible. It wasn't until the end of it that I realized Cookie had been fully engaged and, dare I say, downright enthusiastic about the many random things I was reporting during our meal.

Now, generally speaking, they are an excellent listener and bear witness to my many fascinations with bemused attention on a daily basis, but this was different. This was a specific kind of quality time, as though they were joining me in the nooks and crannies of my mind while I galloped from one topic to another, completely lit up in a wild mix of my fast-paced processing speed and exuberance at a captive audience. It *was* a gift.

You might be thinking, *Her partner listened to her and that was a gift?*

I know, but hear me out. We have two small children. The pandemic has been excruciating. Our days are filled with quick conversations about how to run our home, and then we crumble into exhaustion on the couch. This lunch *was* a gift. It wasn't that they just heard me out. It was that they were pouring enthusiasm into the conversation, that they know me well enough to know that talking about everything I am currently obsessed with while drinking delicious coffee is hands down my favorite thing to do. It was how they rose out of our shared exhaustion to meet the conversation. And it made one hell of a difference to me at that moment.

Your celebrations do not need to be fancy. They can easily be ordinary moments met with extraordinary attention and intention. But regardless of what the celebration encompasses, YOU need to be at the center of it—your joy, pleasure, vitality, exuberance, and deep presence. This gift might not be a noteworthy moment for anyone else, but for me, in that moment, it was exactly what I needed—to feel seen, heard, celebrated, and championed by someone who loves me.

What Is Celebration?

Celebration is a universal need, just as much as safety or belonging. And yet, culturally, we are taught that only certain circumstances merit celebration—birthdays, engagements, promotions, babies, weddings, and graduations—whether or not they pertain to or appeal to us individually. It is little wonder we tend to have a weird relationship with celebration.

This relationship can be especially challenging if you are one of the many whose education about needs was formed in childhoods of pervasive poverty, housing insecurity, food insecurity, or other scarcity of resources. Because these primary safety needs weren't met, we may not have learned what it means to require anything beyond the bare-bones needs of getting by—much less celebration, simply for celebration's sake, unearned and just for the pure joy of it.

What if celebration weren't a specific set of actions? What if, instead, celebration were an intention you hold for yourself and bring to your daily actions instead of waiting until you reach the finish line?

Allie grew up in a family that believed a job well done should be enough of a celebration, reserving these rare moments of revelry for big exciting news, like her sister's promotion, engagement, and birth announcement. Through this lens, Allie's life seemed unimpressive. As a queer, unmarried, and unpartnered waitress with zero desire to have children, she often felt as though the triumphs in her life went unnoticed by everyone in her family. With time, she downplayed these exciting moments, even to herself, because it felt embarrassing to make a big deal out of something when her parents believed she should do something better or start "living up to her potential" in the very prescribed way she was not interested in. Allie felt like a work in progress, and it seemed only big shiny destinations were deserving of applause.

In her free time, Allie was working on a book of short stories. The process was slow, but she loved this creative work. As we began working on weaving celebration into her daily life in imperfect and joyful ways, she decided to incorporate it into her writing process, instead of waiting until the book was finished someday to appreciate the work she was putting into it. She did this in two ways. The first was to make the act of writing feel as celebratory as possible. Before she would dive in, she would clean off her table, set up her computer and journals, and pour herself a cup of coffee. She created a prewriting playlist for herself and danced around in her kitchen while she readied these things, infusing the process of getting to work with as much fun as she could. She also created a map of minimilestones, breaking the project up into many reachable landmarks with the intention of hitting one every other week or so. Allie used these landmarks as opportunities to practice celebrating the small steps in a variety of ways. Some of these celebrations were more substantial—a fancy dinner out, a new sweater, or a gathering with her best friends to cheer her progress—but many were quick, inexpensive, and easily manageable, like painting her nails or watching her favorite movie while eating ice cream.

Let's reclaim these culturally sanctioned ideas about celebration and repurpose this act of revelry, and pleasure by incorporating it into our daily lives in a way that is life-affirming, generative, and sustaining. We yearn to feel appreciated and lifted up. We are aching to break free from a system that deems us worthy of joy only when we hit a sanctioned milestone. This way of approaching our lives keeps us disconnected from our pleasure, waiting to reach the finish line. We withhold our own joy until we earn the promotion, find "the one," or lose the weight, always putting the celebration just out of reach. We feel enormous pressure to celebrate on our birthdays because we perceive it to be our one chance to receive the pleasure or attention we hunger for.

Celebration is not the action itself but the approach and mindset we bring to it. It's a way to thank yourself for all the effort you put into your life on a daily basis, whether or not that effort is noticed, uplifted, or appreciated by anyone else. With this reframe, you might make breakfast in a celebratory way. You might choose to have a dance party in your living room instead of going for a run. You might clean your kitchen in a celebratory way. You might scrub the bathroom in a celebratory way. You might pull out your good china for scrambled eggs in the morning. Give yourself permission to shift celebration from a formal and out-of-reach concept overflowing with the need for external approval and instead, learn to validate and revel in your innate enoughness.

Journal prompts to dive deeper:

Over the course of your life, what have been your favorite celebrations?

What grief do you carry around the idea of celebrating yourself?

What fears do you carry around the idea of celebrating yourself?

What achievements or accomplishments have you been waiting for someone else to notice or recognize?

How might you bring an intention of celebration to a mundane activity in your everyday life?

Healing from the Illusion of the Perfect Celebration

I had been looking forward to it all week, the perfect thing that I had planned, the celebration I had carefully crafted. Over the course of the week, it became more and more important because the more I thought about it, the more it mattered to me. The more it mattered to me, the bigger it became in my mind. Until I woke up sick the morning of. Or the restaurant was closed for renovations. Or my date cancelled. Or the scope of what I planned suddenly wasn't feasible. And I just wanted to sob, overcome with disappointment. My beautiful plan disintegrated as my perfectionism showed herself. *I want it the way I imagined it, or I don't want it at all.*

This is the exact moment when so many of my celebrations crumbled around me. And this is a moment of choice. It is the moment when we can choose to be flexible, softening into what is and adjusting our plans or becoming rigid, angry, and self-pitying. This is the moment when not only the celebration crumbles but everything else crumbles too. How many perfectly imperfect moments of joy do we steel ourselves against, not wanting to receive them unless they are exactly what we expect them to be?

There is healing to be found in making the choice to embrace your perfectly imperfect life and fully embody your perfectly imperfect inner landscape. Your actions, celebrations, and attempts to tend to yourself might fall disappointingly short. You might try something only to realize it was better in theory than it was in reality. Remind yourself that, as with every aspect of your tending, caring for yourself means remaining by your own side during the process of celebrating yourself. Your relationship with yourself doesn't require your perfection. It requires your presence. Your celebrations do not need to be perfect to be deliciously satisfying.

Journal prompts to dive deeper:

What might be possible for you if you were to heal your relationship with celebration?

How do you want to feel when you are celebrating?

What do you appreciate about yourself right now? What tiny celebration could you create for yourself in the next ten minutes to acknowledge it?

If you could create an absolutely perfect celebration, what would that look like? If you put that celebration at the end of a spectrum, what might a micro, everyday expression of that celebration look like?

How much joy can you allow? And what are you willing to do TODAY to feel that way?

 ## Practice: How to Celebrate

At its core, celebration is simple. It requires your willingness and intention to bring more pleasure, joy, and revelry to your current moment.

Start by bringing your awareness to whatever it is you are currently hard at work on. You might be making your way through a project, healing deeply entrenched relationship patterns, learning how to take better care of yourself, tending to small children, figuring out how to create a routine to clean your house more regularly, or building a business. You might be struggling with calling your insurance company about a bill or figuring out how to create boundaries with a family member.

Remind yourself that what you are currently working on is good work. Too often, our daily effort goes unacknowledged or unappreciated, but that does not mean it is unworthy of celebration. It is not possible for someone else to fully understand the extent of energy some of these tasks require of you. Be generous with your declarations by setting the intention to celebrate yourself in small and important ways each day.

One way to practice being your own permission granter and chief celebration coordinator is to set an intention to focus on identifying what YOU find valuable and worthy about yourself each day. Pull out your journal once a day to write three things that you find valuable about yourself or are grateful to yourself for. This practice helps us to move away from only acknowledging our efforts when they are related to external markers of productivity or specific cultural milestones. It helps us to celebrate who we *are* instead of what we've done.

This practice may at times feel uncomfortable and forced. I encourage you to do it anyway because you are more likely to prioritize yourself if you see yourself as valuable and deserving of having your needs met. In this sense, WHY you value yourself becomes the base for HOW you value yourself. If you practice seeing yourself as deserving of celebration, you will be more inclined to celebrate yourself.

Once you get into the habit of appreciating yourself, you are ready to figure out how you might want to acknowledge those efforts. Think back to the information you already unearthed about yourself in previous chapters. How do you best receive love? What lights you up? What is within you that is begging to be lifted up and acknowledged—and how? Root deeply into the relationship you are building as you think about the kind of celebration you might like to welcome into your life, and give yourself permission to experiment here.

Of course, you might still want to do the "traditional" celebration things—throw yourself a party, organize an elaborate dinner, or buy yourself a present—but try getting creative. You could take extra time and care while flossing your teeth or buy a new facial product that smells amazing. When celebrations stop being these large, expensive events in our minds, we can see that a celebration can occur at any moment, in any given setting, with nothing on hand except our bodies and a desire to appreciate ourselves.

This also requires you to tune in to your boundaries and your current resources. Reclaiming time to celebrate yourself is infinitely more challenging if you have been conditioned to believe that you need to work harder than someone else to get ahead. You cannot pull time out of thin air or instantaneously alter a long-standing ethos around effort, but I invite you to consider how you might reallocate a few minutes of time for yourself each day to celebrate your hard work and intrinsic worthiness. How can you make even the most mundane daily activity feel really good for you in particular? How much joy can you allow?

You do not have to wait until you are a finished product, nicely wrapped up and resolved, before you celebrate your hard work. You do not have to wait until someone else tells you that you have done a good job to feel proud. You are allowed to weave celebration into every aspect of your daily life. You are allowed to enjoy the journey between here and where you want to be.

Take a moment to double down on your generosity with your sweet self by making space for celebration.

Start Here

Ask yourself:

What am I proud of having done, accomplished, withstood, or made happen today? Make a list of anything you can think of, no matter how small.

How does it feel to appreciate myself in this way?

Is anything uncomfortable about appreciating myself this way? Why? What stories or beliefs does it kick up?

How am I ready, able, and willing to celebrate myself today? What feels doable?

What will I remind myself of I feel uncomfortable receiving the joy and pleasure of this celebration?

This might look like . . .

If you're at the self-responsibility stage, this might look like sitting with and journaling about why celebration feels uncomfortable. What memories, beliefs, personal myths, or familial legacies does celebrating yourself or allowing yourself to be celebrated dredge up?

If you're at the self-care stage, this might look like bringing a dose of celebration into your regular care routines, like massaging your face for a few minutes as your moisturizer absorbs or getting dressed in your favorite outfit, even if you aren't planning to leave the house.

If you're at the self-trust stage, this might look like stretching to celebrating yourself and your efforts in ways that feel a little edgy or dangerous. Meet yourself in your yearnings and give yourself permission to want what you want—and gently tend to whatever discomfort arises when you do so.

If you're at the self-love stage, this might look like finding hilarious, beautiful, dramatic, or quietly luxurious ways to celebrate yourself regularly. This practice is bolstered by your brilliant awareness of how generative celebration is for you.

If you're at the advocacy stage, this might look like asking for exactly what you want as you welcome others into your celebrations. How do you desire to be lifted up? What would feel fantastic even if it's a bit of an edge for you to ask for it? How do you long to honor a big transition in your life? Lauren was on the precipice of retirement, and she was hurt that after her many years of service, no one in her company seemed to care whether she stayed or left. Sure, they wanted her around because she was reliable and lessened the collective workload, but that paled in comparison to the appreciation and merrymaking she had assumed would herald this transition. After months of resentment, Lauren made a decision to celebrate her lifetime of excellent work in her own way by setting a date to give her notice and booking herself a fabulous vacation to one of her favorite places. It felt uncomfortable to give this gift to herself, but she had to admit that while she was planning it, her resentment started to wane as she imagined how good it would feel to receive this celebration.

Celebration asks us to relish and delight in wonderment as we learn to appreciate ourselves, the humans who surround us, and the natural world we are a small part of. There is nothing frivolous about tending to your need for celebration. It is how you buoy your spirits and appreciate yourself for everything you have lived, are living, and will live through.

An Awkward Celebration Story

At this point in my life, I love to celebrate and be celebrated. But for many years my conditioning would tell me that I was undeserving of my own acceptance and that it was dangerous to celebrate myself too readily or to shine too brightly. It was not safe to celebrate when someone acknowledged my efforts. It was not safe to say "Hey! I did this thing and I am really proud of it," or "I am loving myself today and want to celebrate that." For much of my life, it didn't feel socially safe to even acknowledge liking myself, for fear I would be called out as arrogant, selfish, or self-involved.

After I made the choice not to become a social worker and decided to create my own business instead, I busied myself with creating a new website, a few offerings, a photoshoot that reflected how I felt inside, and my first ebook, *Body Loving Homework*. All summer I worked on these projects in between waitressing shifts and while my partner was at work. I wrote and wrote and wrote until one day my website was finished and my ebook was ready to be released into the world. This felt like a massive accomplishment, both as actual, tangible work done and for the enormous effort it required for me to quiet the self-doubt that roared throughout my consciousness every day I showed up to do the work. I wanted to celebrate.

Yet I felt nauseous at the prospect of being rejected in the face of what I viewed as the largest accomplishment thus far in my life. What if no one understood what I was trying to do? What if no one cared? What if everyone thought having a business on the Internet was a weird and ridiculous thing to do? And underneath it all, what if I asked someone to celebrate with me and they said no?

I know many of us have stood on this precipice, yearning for our efforts to be acknowledged while immobilized by the fear that we won't be met with understanding or appreciation. For much of my life until this point, I had allowed this fear to engulf me. I denied my yearning and pretended it didn't matter, when in fact it mattered deeply.

I picked up the phone and texted a friend: *Hey, my website goes live on Tuesday. Want to go out and grab dinner with me to celebrate?* I pressed send.

I stayed in my seat. I stayed in my body. I remained by my own side, even though I wanted to pick myself last, like the bullies who had made me feel like nothing whenever I showed the merest sparkle of feeling good about myself. I remained by my own side and refused to shame myself for my pride and appreciation for my hard work. I stayed in that seat as the minutes ticked by without a response, refusing to make each passing minute mean I shouldn't have asked. I stayed in that seat, hands tucked under my thighs instead of issuing a follow-up text: *Just kidding. Never mind. It's not that big of a deal. No worries if you're busy.* I stayed in that seat, remaining right by my side, standing firm in my sovereignty as the validator of my needs.

Yes! I would love to.

It was okay to receive too.

⪧ Practice: Trusting and Celebrating New Growth

How do you trust what is newly forming, especially after a life-time of evidence has told you that you can't be trusted? How do you trust you will remain by your own side now, especially when you haven't during particularly painful moments that have come before? How do you keep tending to yourself after you close this book and carry on in your life?

We are conditioned to trust in things that FEEL trustworthy in their steadfast reliability. By contrast, if we are defining reliable as unchanging and static, our inconvenient, messy, human selves are anything but "reliable." Because of this conditioning, we wait to trust ourselves until it feels like a sure thing, placing conditions on our trustworthiness that no real live human could actually meet. This conditioning keeps us from feeling we deserve our own appreciation and keeps us in the limbo of continually practicing new skills without fully believing in our ability to make positive change in our lives.

You are a human and not a robot. Your efforts will be imperfect by design because you are imperfect by design. Your imperfection is not a flaw but a facet of your humanity. The end goal of this book is not to make you into a perfect tender, much less a perfect celebrator. It is to build the bravery to meet yourself exactly where you are in any given moment and remember to ask yourself what you need.

Being a tender steward is not about life-hacking your human inconveniences. It is about reclaiming your body and your life and becoming an active participant in it. It is about connecting deeply with the human beneath your many roles and responsibilities and cherishing yourself for who you are instead of what you do. It is about clearing your desk of distractions and plans you cultivated to spare yourself from having to feel what you feel and instead spending quality time with the parts of you deemed unworthy of attention or kindness. The end goal of this book is to resource you with the necessary tools to help you find your way back home to yourself sooner and easier. It is to help you become intimately familiar with your inner landscape so that you are uniquely equipped to be your own best support system, no matter what needs arise.

START HERE

Pull out a journal and take notes as you contemplate the following questions:

What aspects of my tending feel really solid and dependable right now? What feels shakier and requires more support?

If I cannot rely on myself to do this and everything perfectly, what can I rely on? What DO I trust myself to show up for?

How will I ritualize the practice of checking in with myself each day so that it becomes a natural part of my routine?

What warning signs remind me I am in need of my own care? Can I pull my list out and put it somewhere I will see often?

How can I remind myself to approach myself with curiosity and creativity whenever I notice there is something I need to take responsibility for?

What is my essential self-care routine right now? What three things am I ready, able, and willing to commit to doing each day to support myself?

How am I defining trustworthiness, and am I making room for my own humanity in that definition?

How will I celebrate my growth without constantly comparing myself to my unrealistic expectations?

This practice is an invitation to plan to get lost along your path. Plan that you will forget your tending and think about how you will reconnect with your needs when you inevitably lose your way. Plan that you will screw this up because you are gloriously human.

Ask yourself: *How can I support myself to continue making my tending a priority for me?*

THIS MIGHT LOOK LIKE . . .

If you're at the self-responsibility stage, this might look like putting a little notebook on your bedside table, and each night before you go to bed taking a moment to record one little thing you notice you did differently that day.

If you're at the self-care stage, this might look like leaning in to the empowerment of taking imperfect action and feeling enthusiastic about continuing to take imperfect actions in your life.

If you're at the self-trust stage, this might look like developing a greater understanding of what you personally require to show up for yourself with consistency, openness, bravery, and compassion—and be mindful to keep doing that on purpose.

If you're at the self-love stage, this might look like pausing each day to acknowledge and celebrate your efforts regardless of the outcome.

If you're at the advocacy stage, this might look like sharing about your new growth with the people in your life. Tell them what you are proud of. Ask for support for what still feels wobbly or uncertain. You do not have to do this work in a silo. You can ask for and receive external support as you navigate implementing some of the changes you are experimenting with. Rachel had been deepening into the work of learning how to set boundaries with her family of origin. This work felt overwhelming as she was very close to her large family and worried she might be cast out for wanting and needing something different from her siblings. When she had worked up to the stage of verbalizing her needs, she shared what she was about to do with her close group of friends so that they could cheer her on and remind her WHY she wanted to set these boundaries. Rachel ached to have closer and more intimate relationships with the members of her family, something that wasn't possible when she was working overtime to keep the peace. The plus side was that because she had asked for their support, her friends were also there for the moments of discomfort when her new boundaries weren't well received or faced a certain amount of pushback. These friends were able to remind Rachel that there *were* people who accepted and loved her for who she was, and these reminders gave her the confidence to begin shifting the dynamics in her familial relationships as she allowed more of her truest self to be witnessed.

Walking Up the Golden Staircase

In 1983, psychology theorists James Prochaska and Carlo DiClemente created a transtheoretical model called *Stages of Change* to describe the process a human undertakes when creating intentional change in their lives.[1] These stages bring the individual through precontemplation, contemplation, preparation, action, maintenance, relapse, and back again to precontemplation. When using this model to think about creating effective change, it can be useful to imagine the two-dimensional cycle occurring in a spiral, where each rotation occurs at a higher elevation on the vertical plane. In doing this work, I like to imagine moving through these stages as walking up a golden spiral staircase. We are always in the process of moving between these stages, readying ourselves to take meaningful action in our lives as we gather data from our mistakes and fine-tune our next iteration. What is particularly important about this model is that it gives us a grounding point when we encounter triggers and old wounds that feel devastatingly familiar. We might be heartbroken to realize that even with all of our hard work, we are still grappling with the same issue.

What is remarkably heartening about Prochaska and DiClemente's theory is that the concept of relapse is baked into the model. It is anticipated that humans will move through some kind of upset, perceived failure, or disappointment, and that its presence doesn't mean we are doing it wrong or will never be able to create meaningful change. This relapse and the data gained from the experience are essential for crafting your next iteration in a way that is a better fit for you specifically. Seen this way, it's not only a good thing but also critical to your deepening into relationship with yourself. And building celebration into the process makes it that much sweeter and more effective!

Return for a moment to your inner landscape, the wild expanse of internal territory that you have been getting to know and learning to tend throughout this book. While reading these pages, you have worked to familiarize yourself with your surroundings and to take responsibility for being the tender steward of this patch of earth and lovingly care for it in whatever way it requires. You have padded around here, barefoot and rooting into your unique humanity as you acquaint yourself with your surroundings. You have learned to appreciate this landscape instead of forfeiting your precious time here wishing it were more like someone else's inner landscape or comparing it to an arbitrary ideal you were conditioned to value over your own innate wildness. You have tended to your gardens, planting seeds and watering plants, speaking to them and yourself kindly to foster an environment fertile for growth.

The recognition of peace here within your wilderness is a celebration. The harvest of your fruits and vegetables is a celebration. Each and every bloom is a celebration. Receiving and appreciating your efforts is a celebration. Fully embodying your existence is a celebration. You do not require anyone's permission to make your home here, surrounded by your own lush wilderness and fragile growth. You do not require anyone's permission to root in deeply here, dedicating yourself to yourself for the duration of your life. You do not need to wait for external approval to bloom here, and you certainly don't require anyone else's validation to stand in your sovereign, benevolent leadership.

Put yourself in charge. Choose your celebrations. Decide to celebrate yourself generously. Find ways to celebrate each stage in your cycle, ushering yourself up your golden staircase with a standing ovation and raucous revelry. This progress is yours to cherish and receive.

Commitments to My Need for Celebration

— Celebration is a need. It's not negotiable or something I can earn or something that has to wait until my birthday. Giving myself permission to celebrate is a sacred act of self-love.

— Bringing celebration into every moment of my life—not as an act per se but as a mindset and approach to living—is an act of gratitude to myself.

— I do not have to do it perfectly. In fact, I can't. I choose to resist putting so much pressure on individual acts of celebration that they become chores.

— Celebrations can be tiny and private. Scrubbing my bathroom can be just as celebratory as having a party. And if I have a habit of downplaying my celebrations, it might be time to try something bigger.

— In celebrating, I show myself love and concretize my legacy of trust with myself. I will be doing this work until the day I die. Celebrating each iteration is in and of itself an act of tending.

Reverence for Your Life

I STARTED THIS BOOK with a dedication and prayer for my daughters, that they would always know what they needed and have the courage to ask for it. That's my deepest wish for you as well—that this book emboldens and strengthens you to know what you need and have the courage to ask for it.

Through this work, I hope you learn how to live more flexibly, resilient in the face of inevitable uncertainty and with a loose grasp on the outcome because it no longer defines your worth. I hope you are able to embody the width and breadth of your life in a deeply human and unmistakably ordinary way, braiding pleasure and joy into every aspect of your existence.

This work is under no circumstances optional.

Taking care of yourself is easier when you have time, space, resources, and privilege to do it.

Taking care of yourself is essential when you do not have the time, space, resources, and privilege to do it.

You are allowed to be who and how you are. The world is made better by witnessing and engaging with you in your fullness. Your relationships are better for it. Your communities are better for it. Your ability to contribute to the world—from the deeply rooted place of knowing the edges of your capacity and honoring your own delightful preferences for sharing your gifts—is better for it.

To welcome yourself into every corner of your life, you must build your vocabulary for what you are aching for, naming your specific needs and partnering with the part of you that has been unable to conform or be forgotten in the busyness of daily life. Meet that ache for nourishment with the skills and the tangible support offered in this book. Let these discussions be a jumping-off point for you as you deepen into the life-altering reservoir of permission available when you show up for yourself in ways you may have never thought possible. I hope practicing the exercises will continue to support you to bridge the gap between your current life experiences and the life you are only beginning to allow yourself to dream of.

I opened the introduction with the story of me on the couch holding my new baby because this was the moment that broke me open to the truth that I had no idea what I needed or how to ask for it, even after so much time and self-work. In subtle and insidious ways, the underpinnings of my life continued to be constructed in such a way that they looked impressive, earned me belonging, supported the people around me, and were in large part safe—but they weren't true for me. I was still sacrificing my time, energy, and desires whenever I suspected anyone needed me. I was still holding myself to an inhumane standard.

Taking care of myself looks different now, while mothering two children under six during a pandemic while running a business, writing a book, reorganizing our family unit to care for a family friend with cancer, and trying to keep my marriage alive. It is found in reclaimed moments in between activities, remembering to water and feed myself, and while watching *Schitt's Creek* on my phone in the bathroom as I floss my teeth during a five-minute spot of solitude and joy in a day packed full of emotional overload.

Caring for yourself is essential, even and especially in the moments when you tell yourself you couldn't possibly do so.

There are many, many loads of laundry now. My kids routinely stay home for weeks on end because they have a cold. There are tense moments with my spouse about who gets to take the dog for a walk and who has to vacuum the thousands of seeds our daughter just knocked out of her sensory bin, as we both try to be the humans we are while also showing up for everything we have built and care about deeply.

I have been stopped in my tracks again and again as I bear witness to the gaps between what I have been allowing myself and what the soft animal of my body longs for, as Mary Oliver so aptly described it.

Perhaps you've experienced a moment like that. Or perhaps you were drawn to this work because you are exhausted from the consequences of putting yourself last, playing small, and pretending to be someone you aren't. Perhaps it is a combination of these things.

In each of those moments, I have noticed myself wanting to take my resentment and frustration out on the people around me for not supporting me or showing me I mattered to them. And every single time that anger arrived, I realized I hadn't been mattering to or honoring myself. I hadn't been honest with myself about my capacity or my needs. I had fallen back into a pattern of exploiting myself, over-serving in an attempt to work my way to rest when it was rest I deeply ached for.

This work is about mattering to yourself.

It is about developing a relationship with yourself where you feel seen, heard, and held. Where your needs are lovingly coaxed forward and met as regularly and often as you can. Where you become an active participant in your inner world. Where your needs, wants, preferences, boundaries, and conditions for thriving are at the epicenter of every word you utter internally and externally and every decision you make.

Over the course of this book, I shared stories—my own and others—about grappling with our inherent neediness, voracious hunger to be loved, and deep fears about renegotiating the boundaries we require to exist and thrive.

I wrote this book for myself first. This is the book I needed ten years ago when I fell into the chasm between my true, human self and the expectations I had been holding for myself.

For the little girl both needing to disappear to feel safe and wanting to be found to feel loved.

For the kid wanting to be nurtured instead of relegated to the parts of the sport she was okay at.

For the college student realizing for the first time that the affection she was settling for was so much less than the love she required.

For the sleep-deprived new mother grappling with postpartum anxiety and depression.

For the woman deeply craving celebration but terrified that shining too brightly will threaten her carefully pieced-together sense of belonging.

But I wrote this book for you too, for the parts of you that have been longing to be known, tenderly held, and boldly expressed.

You matter. Your needs matter.

I believe in you.

I am planting seeds in my inner landscape. At first, I pressed each seed carefully into the waiting earth. I measured the space between seeds. I charted my garden with intricate patterns and plans, carefully controlling the bloom.

But with each seed I feel my body loosening. I feel the knot in the pit of my stomach relax. With each seed I am a little less concerned about the outcome. Once, the flower was the prize. It was the tangible marker that told the world I was a good gardener. That I could be trusted with the most fragile seeds. That I was accomplished.

With each seed I become a little bit more reckless. I am enjoying myself now. I am working up a bit of a sweat with my hands in the dirt and the sun on my face. The more I enjoy the process of planting the seeds, the less concerned I am about the flowering plant itself.

This is trust. This is blooming within.

I no longer need to control each and every variable. I no longer need to white-knuckle my planting because I understand in earnest that when I am working with a living breathing thing—whether it be seed or dream or idea—I alone am not responsible for the outcome.

It is my job to show up here. To plant the seeds. To follow through in watering the earth every so often. To do the best that I can with the tools I have on hand. It is my job to pour myself into the process with messy joy, space for heartache, and blooming celebration. It is my job not to hold anything back. It is my job to be here now.

For a moment I have an inkling to throw my head back and start to spin, arms outstretched and taking up space here on this patch of earth. I get just a flash of how fun it might be to sow my garden this way, spinning arms and whirling feet as seeds fly from my hands and land in just the right place throughout my yard.

What if I override the voice that tells me this is simply not how things are done? What if I trust my heart to guide me?

And so I plant my garden—skirt spinning, dirt-speckled, and giddy with exhilaration.

Acknowledgments

IN A WORLD of self-proclaimed "self-made" humans, it feels essential to share openly about how we make things, our support systems, and the people whose labor freed up our time to write. I had immense practical and emotional support in writing this book, and it made a remarkable difference. Following the themes of this book, gaining access to this support required me to learn how to figure out specifically what I needed, ask for it, and be open to receive it, even when it was uncomfortable or felt like an enormous imposition on the people around me.

For Cookie: Thank you for caring for the children and our home so that I could write this book. Thank you for knowing that it was a lifelong dream of mine and conspiring to make it happen with me. Thank you for the emotional labor of listening to me process this process. Thank you for knowing yourself so deeply and being a teacher for me as I have come to know myself over the last fourteen years. I love you.

For Nola: Your support brought this book to life. Thank you for sitting next to me while I wrote the shitty first draft, for feeding me snacks, for talking to me endlessly about this project over the span of three years, for editing those first stream-of-consciousness pages with such grace and brilliance, and for helping me dismantle and reconstruct that final book proposal, sentence by sentence. Thank you. I am incredibly grateful for your patience and ability to care for this project even in the moments when I was too scared to.

For my parents, Kathe Izzo and Wendelin Glatzel: Thank you for raising me to believe deeply in my ability to create things that don't yet exist in the world around me. For providing me with so many of the tools that have grown into facets of this work. For providing tangible support with my children so I could carve out time to get these words onto paper. And to my mother, specifically, for teaching me to write. I love you so much.

For Becca Piastrelli: Thank you for becoming such an incredible champion of my work. Thank you for your steadfast support, encouragement, and generosity with sharing my work and helping me get it into the right hands.

For Rachel Allen: Working with you on the draft of this book was such an utter delight and profound gift. I deeply appreciate your care and editing prowess. THANK YOU.

For Claire, Kait, Lesley, Dianna, and Julian: The dinner you threw for me and this book was the single most favorite celebration of my life. The memory of it will live in my heart for a very, very long time.

For Richelle: Working with you on my book proposal was an absolute joy. I cannot say enough about your vision, charisma, and gloriously human leadership style. I feel very lucky to have you in my orbit.

For my agent, Wendy Sherman: Thank you for taking a chance on me, and for believing so deeply in my work. It has been such an honor to work with you to bring this book to life.

For Haven: I have had the kind words you wrote about *Needy* in the offer from Sounds True posted above my desk since you wrote them and feel so grateful to get to work with an editor who is such an advocate for this work. Thank you for your vision of what that first book proposal could become, and thank you for standing behind this project.

For Sarah, Jade, and the team at Sounds True: I am incredibly grateful for the kindness and diligence that you poured into this book over the last year. Thank you for treating these tender words with so much love. I am so grateful for you all.

For the Mavens: Thank you for holding me during a time when I was deep in the thick of holding myself, for reminding me who I am, and for championing my work. I carry your kind words with me, always.

For the *Needy* early readers: Daren Loughrey, Sarah Flick, Andréa Ranae, Hannah Marcotti, Persephone Brown, Staci McGowan, Susannah Slocum, Justine Taormino, Kate Sheehan, Mariglynn Edlins, Amy Bouldin, and my dearest sister, Jules—your feedback was essential in helping to shape this book. I will forever value your kind, attentive notes and consider myself so damn lucky to have you in my life.

For Bear Hebert's writing group: Grace, Fanny, Joanna, Sara, Peter, Angeliska, Will, Jennifer, Nicole, Amanda, Meghan, Rebecca, Alex, Quincy, Helen, Kate, Hope, Kendra, Darla, Jenny, Sarah—thank you. So many of these words were written while spending time with you over Zoom, and that cozy coworking container made all of the difference in the world. Bear, I am incredibly grateful to you for inviting me to join your community during a time when everything felt so isolating. Thank you.

To all of my clients, friends, family, and loved ones over the last ten years: This work has been stretched and formed in part by each and every one of you. This work and my own personal work are deeply relational. This wouldn't exist without your presence in my life. Thank you, for you.

To Rachel Germann, Liz Grant, and Rebekka Ellman: Thank you for supporting me in caring for my physical, emotional, and energetic bodies during the process of working on this book. Your care made me feel whole, rooted, and capable during the creative roller coaster of this project and enabled me to nourish this work sustainably.

To Helen Jane Long: Thank you for the gift of your music, nearly every single word in this book was written while listening to *Live at St. James, London*.

For David Tobin: You are so loved.

Additional Reading List

Adult Children of Emotionally Immature Parents: How to Heal from Distant, Rejecting, or Self-Involved Parents by Lindsay C. Gibson

Adventures in Opting Out: A Field Guide to Leading an Intentional Life by Cait Flanders

All About Love: New Visions by bell hooks

Already Enough: A Path to Self-Acceptance by Lisa Olivera

The Art of Receiving and Giving: The Wheel of Consent by Betty Martin, DC, with Robyn Dalzen

Belly of the Beast: The Politics of Anti-Fatness as Anti-Blackness by Da'Shaun L. Harrison

Black Women Thriving Report: 2022 by Ericka Hines, JD, and Mako Fitts Ward, PhD (a project of Every Level Leadership)

The Body Is Not an Apology, Second Edition: The Power of Radical Self-Love by Sonya Renee Taylor

The Book of Boundaries: Set the Limits That Will Set You Free by Melissa Urban

Burnout: The Secret to Unlocking the Stress Cycle by Emily Nagoski, PhD, and Amelia Nagoski, DMA

The Care We Dream Of: Liberatory and Transformative Approaches to LGBTQ+ Health by Zena Sharman

Care Work: Dreaming Disability Justice by Leah Lakshmi Piepzna-Samarasinha

Desire, Mystery, and Belonging by Sarah Flick, MD

Discovering the Inner Mother: A Guide to Healing the Mother Wound and Claiming Your Personal Power by Bethany Webster

Do Better: Spiritual Activism for Fighting and Healing from White Supremacy by Rachel Ricketts

Fearing the Black Body: The Racial Origins of Fat Phobia by Sabrina Strings

Getting to Center: Pathways to Finding Yourself Within the Great Unknown by Marlee Grace

Grieving While Black: An Antiracist Take on Oppression and Sorrow by Breeshia Wade

I'm Still Here: Black Dignity in a World Made for Whiteness by Austin Channing Brown

My Grandmother's Hands: Racialized Trauma and the Pathway to Mending Our Hearts and Bodies by Resmaa Menakem

Pleasure Activism: The Politics of Feeling Good by adrienne maree brown

Reclaiming Body Trust: A Path to Healing & Liberation by Hilary Kinavey and Dana Sturtevant

Rest Is Resistance: A Manifesto by Tricia Hersey

Root and Ritual: Timeless Ways to Connect to Land, Lineage, Community, and the Self by Becca Piastrelli

Sacred Rest: Recover Your Life, Renew Your Energy, Restore Your Sanity by Saundra Dalton-Smith, MD

Set Boundaries, Find Peace: A Guide to Reclaiming Yourself by Nedra Glover Tawwab

The Seven Circles: Indigenous Teachings for Living Well by Chelsey Luger and Thosh Collins

Trans Bodies, Trans Selves: A Resource by and for Transgender Communities by Laura Erickson-Schroth

Undrowned: Black Feminist Lessons from Marine Mammals by Alexis Pauline Gumbs

You Are the Medicine: 13 Moons of Indigenous Wisdom, Ancestral Connection, and Animal Spirit Guidance by Asha Frost

You Have the Right to Remain Fat by Virgie Tovar

Notes

Epigraph

1. Mary Oliver, "Wild Geese," *Dream Work* (New York: The Atlantic Monthly Press, 1986), 14.

Chapter 5: Trust

1. Brené Brown, *Rising Strong: How the Ability to Reset Transforms the Way We Live, Love, Parent, and Lead* (New York: Random House, 2015).

Chapter 10: Celebration

1. J. O. Prochaska and C. C. DiClemente, "Stages and Processes of Self-Change of Smoking: Toward an Integrative Model of Change," *Journal of Consulting and Clinical Psychology* 51 no. 3 (1983): 390–395, doi.org/10.1037/0022-006X.51.3.390.

About the Author

MARA GLATZEL (she/her) is a writer, intuitive coach, and podcast host—but really, she is a needy human who helps other needy humans stop abandoning themselves and start taking up space in their own lives.

In a world teeming with self-care gurus and bubble bath–laden listicles geared toward prioritizing the self-care that helps you produce more, Mara will never sell you a quick fix and will forever champion the resiliency and inherent worthiness of your radiant humanity. Instead of urging you to continue looking outside yourself for answers, Mara's paradigm-shifting work will teach you to turn inward toward yourself, again and again.

Mara is a queer, femme mother of two, recovering control freak, and human who deeply understands the impulse to relegate her needs to the bottom of a very long to-do list in an attempt to prove her worth. She lives on the tip of Cape Cod with her partner, children, and rambunctious puppy, Lady.

Learn more about her work at maraglatzel.com.

About Sounds True

SOUNDS TRUE is a multimedia publisher whose mission is to inspire and support personal transformation and spiritual awakening. Founded in 1985 and located in Boulder, Colorado, we work with many of the leading spiritual teachers, thinkers, healers, and visionary artists of our time. We strive with every title to preserve the essential "living wisdom" of the author or artist. It is our goal to create products that not only provide information to a reader or listener but also embody the quality of a wisdom transmission.

For those seeking genuine transformation, Sounds True is your trusted partner. At SoundsTrue.com you will find a wealth of free resources to support your journey, including exclusive weekly audio interviews, free downloads, interactive learning tools, and other special savings on all our titles.

To learn more, please visit SoundsTrue.com/freegifts or call us toll-free at 800.333.9185.